salt

the essential guide to cooking
with the most important
ingredient in your kitchen

salt

leslie bilderback

photographs by teri lyn fisher

St. Martin's Griffin
New York

www.stmartins.com

Designed by Elizabeth Van Itallie

Production Manager: Lisa Viviani Goris

The Library of Congress Cataloging-in-Publication Data is available
upon request.

ISBN 978-1-250-08871-0 (paper over board)
ISBN 978-1-250-08872-7 (e-book)

Our books may be purchased in bulk for promotional, educational,
or business use. Please contact your local bookseller or the Macmillan
Corporate and Premium Sales Department at 1-800-221-7945, extension
5442, or by e-mail at MacmillanSpecialMarkets@macmillan.com.

First Edition: September 2016

10 9 8 7 6 5 4 3 2 1

This book is dedicated to
Bill, Emma, and Claire, who
were with me on that first
amazing salt mine tour,
and slid down the banister
with me. Thanks for trying
all the weird salt with open
minds and big smiles.

contents

OPPOSITE: INFUSED ASIAN SALTS

introduction

When my girls were still in high school, we took a family vacation to Austria. We took the obligatory *Sound of Music* Tour, then headed up into the mountains of neighboring Berchtesgaden, just over the border in Germany. Our schedule allowed for either a tour of the Eagle's Nest, or a tour of a salt mine. We chose the salt mine, despite the eyeball-rolling of my teenage girls, who weren't so much interested in World War II history as they were the busload of German boys headed in that direction. (It was a veritable Rolf smorgasbord.)

That tour of the Berchtesgaden's main salt mine turned out to be the most amazing thing we did during the entire two-week trip, and the one thing about that summer we still all talk about. After donning matching safety jumpsuits, we boarded tiny trains that chugged us deep into the mountain. We sped (and I mean *sped*) through tunnels that left very little head clearance for my 6-foot-1-inch husband. We passed interpretive historical signs and markers, mannequins decked out in old-timey miner garb, and video explanations of the mining process. When it was time to continue down to the lower level of the mine, we did it the old-fashioned way—all four of us stacked together on a banister. What a kick! It wasn't so much thrilling as crazily unexpected—and a dash bizarre. The tour culminated in a boat ride across Mirror Lake. That's a lake inside the mountain created by the mining process. While it is cool enough just being on a lake inside a mountain, they added music and a laser light show that rivaled any Pink Floyd *Laserium* I saw in the '70s.

As a chef I was familiar with a few artisan salts. I occasionally used *fleur de sel* or Maldon sea salt in a finishing application. I was particular about my use of kosher salt in the kitchen, and routinely forced my students to taste it (much to their displeasure) and compare the flavor of kosher salt with the table salt they were used to using. But it was not until that Austrian trip that I really understood the true nature of salt. Over time I realized that I have been sadly, saltily ignorant.

The mining of salt, in particular, was an abstract concept to me. I recognized its existence, thanks to the mule boys of Pinocchio's Pleasure Island. But, up until that trip, I had really only thought of salt as a product of the sea—which, of course, it is. It just so happens that many of the seas are long gone, their remnants trapped in mountains.

I ended up tasting and buying a number of Bavarian salts on that trip, and have since become a salt collector—indeed, a salt nerd extraordinaire—a trait that you can now benefit from.

PART 1

SALTS OF THE WORLD

A BRIEF EXPLANATION OF SALT

This book is about cooking with salt. But my philosophy has always been that knowing the history of a food makes cooking it much more enjoyable. And for professional chefs, not knowing a food's history makes you a bad practitioner. The history of salt has already been well documented in several best-selling tomes, with which I am loath to compete. (If you have not already read it, run out and buy *Salt: A World History* by Mark Kurlansky.) With that in mind, however, please allow me to offer just a few facts that will make your salty exploration more meaningful.

SALT AND ECONOMICS

Salt has been important to humankind for millennia—probably since the first civilizations sprung up along the edges of deserts spotted with salt deposits. Salt not only immediately made everything tastier, it became vital to food preservation (as you will learn in the section Curing with Salt). It also became important in the production of leather, textiles, and as a pain remedy. Human health depends on salt, too. And although early peoples couldn't have known to what extent, it was likely clear that life was better when they had salt. Thus began the economic chapter of salt's history.

Early wars were fought for salty territories, and saltworks have been key targets in wartime, including during the American Civil War. Slaves were traded for it (if they were worth their salt). Roman legionnaires were probably not really paid with it, although it makes a good story about the origin of the word *salary*. Salt taxes were levied in most countries; the first we know of were in China in the third century BC. Salt became an essential commodity that offered great power to those that controlled it—a fact that fueled more than one revolution (Gandhi's Salt March, the French Gabelle, The Moscow Salt Riot). Revenue from salt taxes funded everything from the British Monarchy to the Erie Canal.

The salt trade plied notably, and early, by the Phoenicians, helped create new roads, trade routes, ports, and cities. The *Via Salaria* is considered by some historians to be the reason Rome exists at all. First it delivered the Sabines to the salt pans of Ostia (Porta Salaria at the Aurelian Walls), then it extended out to the Adriatic. Cheshire County in England has been an important salt-producing region since medieval times, and Liverpool became hugely important (long before the Beatles) as the main conduit of salt from Cheshire. Munich rose to power by controlling the trade of salt from Salzburg (literally "salt mountain"). Poland's wealth and prominence in the sixteenth century were similarly due to profit from local salt mines.

SALT AND SPIRITUALITY

It should be no surprise that something wielding so much power and wealth would, eventually, be given spiritual significance. The Old and New Testaments repeatedly use salt as a parable (Lot's wife, salt of the earth, *sal*vation). The evil of Judas is telegraphed as he knocks over the salt in Da Vinci's depiction of the *Last Supper*. Salt was used in Greek ritual sacrifice and Jewish temple offerings. Buddhists use it to repel bad spirits, and, as such, it is a very important element of a sumo wrestling match. Shinto use salt to purify, Indians offer it as a symbol of good luck, and natives of the American Southwest worshipped the Salt Mother.

I can understand the negative connotations of salt. My nicked hands sting with every salty application. And as a kid, my mom let me pour salt on the slugs that were destroying our garden. Salt has been used to destroy agricultural land, and also as a defense against icy roads. Still, despite the havoc salt can wreak, it remains to me a symbol of love. Food is made better by salt, and by association, so are meals. And the better the meal, the more love gathers at the table. Good food brings my kids home, and for that I am eternally grateful to salt.

Eating together. Brotherly and sisterly love. Salt is awesome.

WHAT IS SALT?

Salt comes from the sea. Both the seas we have today, and ancient seas long gone. We extract it from bodies of salt water, from the center of mountains, or from dried-up deserts, all of which contain the minerals of the sea, including NaCL, sodium chloride—a.k.a. salt.

The majority of the world's salt production is performed by a handful of companies, primarily in China, the United States, and India, with smaller but still ample production happening in Germany, Austria, Canada, Mexico, Chile, and Brazil. Most of it comes from rock salt mining (about 70 percent), and the rest is harvested from seawater and lake pans. But these industrial giants, though impressive, are not what this book is about. We are, as culinarians, more interested in the smaller producers—and there are plenty. Almost every country on Earth has some type of salt production, if only to supply the local population. To know and appreciate local salt artisans will, in turn, help us know and appreciate their local history, cuisine, and culture. And an appreciation of another culture is the first step in understanding and tolerance.

In other words, salt is totally the gateway to world peace.

So, in that spirit, let's learn a little more about salt.

SEA SALT

As I mentioned, all salt comes from the sea. But it is the salt from our modern, liquid seas that is generally called *sea salt*. To reveal its salt, the seawater must be evaporated. This can be done in several ways. Simply boiling the seawater is a tried-and-true method. I did this in my kitchen with Pacific water from up the California coast. (Not LA water—that would be gross.) Boiling seawater has a long tradition. You can visit Seaside, Oregon, where Lewis and Clark's Corps of Discovery boiled seawater for two months straight, producing almost 30 gallons of salt for their trip home. (This scene is reenacted for your amusement every August.) A similar method of salt production began at Cape Cod after a Revolutionary War embargo was instituted on salt imported from Liverpool. By the mid-1800s Cape Cod was home to at least 700 saltworks. The Vikings poured salt water over burning logs, then scraped up the salt when the fires extinguished. In the Middle Ages the salt makers on the Danish Læsø Island boiled salt water in hundreds of wood-burning salt kilns. Precolonial Mesoamericans were harvesting salt in a similar manner from the sea in coastal Michoacán and Colima. The Romans boiled salt in lead pans, which have been found by archeologists throughout the Empire. Coastal European Bronze Age cultures boiled salt water in ceramic jars known as *briquetage* (see Glossary page 198). Traces of these ceramics have turned up far afield, pointing to a vast salt trade network. Briquetage dating to the early Neolithic age have been found in Romania, which is currently considered the earliest known salt production facility, dating to 6050 BC.

In warmer regions of the world salt was harvested using only natural sun and wind to evaporate the water. Many of these facilities still function, and have boomed in recent years, thanks in part to culinary demand. The first salt to receive widespread culinary attention comes from Guérande, on the Atlantic coast of France. The salt in this region has been harvested in the same manner since the Middle Ages. Shallow pools sit in the sun, and when the time is right (May through September) the delicate top layer of crystals is removed by hand with a specialized wooden rake. This layer is called "flower of the sea," or *fleur de sel* in French. Despite what they will tell you in Guérande, a good flower of the sea does not need to be French. Perfectly wonderful versions are created along many other coastlines—all along the coast of Brittany, in the Algarve region of Portugal, the Ebro Delta in Spain, the province of Trapani, Sicily, the Lagoon of Cuyutlán in Mexico, and in Phetchaburi, Thailand, you can find unique flowers of the sea. The natural evaporation of these salts typically yields a lower-sodium and higher-mineral content than rock or boiled salt. The historic evaporation pools and the traditional methods of harvesting by hand are appealing to consumers interested in artisan techniques, landing these salts in the top dining rooms of the world.

After flower of the sea is harvested, there is still residual salt that sinks to the bottom of the pools. This is called "grey salt," or *sel gris* in French. Its grayish color comes from contact with the silt at the bottom of the salt pan. More moist and oceanic in flavor, grey salt is cheaper, too. As a result it is more commonly used by chefs as an everyday salt.

In cooler regions, production may start with the sun, then finish evaporating in covered salt sun houses (as is done by Maine Sea Salt Company, and San Juan Island Sea Salt in Washing-

ton State), or through the application of heat, either by fire (as in Japanese *agehama* style salt, Maldon of Essex, Halen Môn in Wales, and Læsø Island in Denmark). The technique can be carefully regulated to produce specific sizes of salt grains, from very fine, to coarse, to large delicate pyramidal crystals.

These coastal saltworks were historically set up in areas with a coastline that was inset or otherwise protected from the raging sea. They would have needed a steady fuel source nearby with which to dry the salt—either a reliable sun, wood, or another cheap fuel source. It also helped to have another industry nearby that relied on the salt, such as tanning or livestock (salt is used in meat preservation).

Some of these saltworks remain, and their daily salt-making tasks are carried out with reverence. Other sites use the same basic technique to push millions of tons of salt around on giant mountains with tractors onto barges for transport around the world. These large operations fulfill mostly industrial use, but also supply what we know as table salt—something from which you will soon be forever free.

ROCK SALT

Rock salt, mountain salt, mined salt, fossil salt, and marine fossil salt are all names for the same thing—inland salt. Not only inland from the sea, but literally in-the-land. How did salt get into the earth, you ask? There were once bodies of saltwater connected to the sea by narrow channels. Eventually, the sea connection was cut off and over time evaporation concentrated the water's salt content. The salt settled to the bottom, layering over time with other minerals. (They fall to the bottom in order of solubility,

so geologists can predict the presence of salt based on the presence of these other mineral layers.) As geological activity shifted the Earth's crust, salt deposits moved, thrusting upward into mountain ranges, or making other unique formations, like salt domes and salt walls. Most of these primordial oceans are found in the Northern Hemisphere.

If salt deposits found their way to the surface, they were dissolved by rain or groundwater. This salty runoff then flowed down, creating underground brine, also known as saline springs. It is these springs that attracted early humans, and most early settlements were situated around such salty sources. Solnitsata, Bulgaria, the oldest town in Europe (a title that is not without controversy) was established around such briny springs between 4700 and 4200 BC.

SALT LAKES

Salty bodies of water still exist in some parts of the world. These nondraining, stationary waters are found in dry areas with limited rainfall. The water evaporates faster than it is replenished, and so the salt content increases. You can visit some of these lakes—Lake Assal in Djibouti, the Great Salt Lake in Utah, the Dead Sea, Garabogazköl, a lagoon at the eastern edge of the Caspian Sea—and float effortlessly in their thick salty waters. Alas, you probably cannot visit the saltiest body of water in the world, Don Juan Pond in Antarctica, which has a sodium content of 40 percent. (However, I highly recommend you Google it, so we can get to the bottom of its name.) Salt lakes still provide salt in some areas, and are often coveted for their culinary and healing properties.

SALT DESERTS, MARSHES, AND DUNE FIELDS

When evaporation of a salt lake has exceeded precipitation over millions of years, a salt desert (also called salt pan, or salt flat) occurs. Found primarily between mountain ranges, the most famous salt flats include Bolivia's Salar de Uyuni, Namibia's Etosha pan, and Utah's Bonneville Flats. These sites are host to both the salt industry and tourists, due in large part to an unusual eco-diversity (flamingos are a common sight, as they are specially adapted to salty water), and a huge flat landscape that calls out to speed racers.

Some locations, like the *sabkhas* of Tunisia and Algeria, are considered salt marshes, because they fill temporarily with several feet of water during the region's rainy season, making them impassable. Dune fields, like those found in the Empty Quarter of Saudi Arabia, occur when evaporation leaves tiny pools behind. Water from rain or underground springs fills in the space between crests of dunes. Salt is extracted from locations such as these by cutting blocks out of the crust, or, in some cases, blowing it out with explosives. Desert salt has long been a commodity. Early trade routes were established from North Africa across the Sahara to the Niger River, through which salt could be exchanged ounce for ounce with gold.

Overlooking Bolivia's Uyuni Salt Desert is the Hotel de Sal Luna Salada. There you can sit at the salt bar sipping salty drinks as you look out over the salt flats, then retire to your salt bed for what will be, no doubt, salty dreams.

SALT MINES

The world's oldest known salt mine is in Hallstatt, Austria, where mining began during the late Neolithic period. You can visit the museum there and see the Neolithic axes and Bronze Age hammers and picks used to remove the salt. Today, salt mines extract salt one of two ways. It can be cut and blasted out, or it can be extracted through controlled solution mining, which is the more common method today. Holes are drilled into the rock salt deposits and water is pumped in. The rock dissolves into a briny solution that is pumped out and evaporated. You can see this in action, because many of the world's salt mines have been given second lives as tourist attractions. The Khewra Salt Mine in Pakistan is a major draw. It was supposedly discovered by Bucephalous (Alexander the Great's horse) who wouldn't stop licking the rocks. There, you can see a number of artistic salt constructs, including a salt mosque and a salt Great Wall of China. In Poland, the Wieliczka Mine, which produced table salt from the thirteenth century until 2007, has a salt "Last Supper." In Kansas you can visit the Strataca underground salt museum, a site discovered by mistake in the 1880s while drilling for oil. There kids can have underground campouts, and adults can participate in Mine Murder Mystery dinners. And in Berchtesgaden you can slide down the banister and float across the laser-embellished Mirror Lake.

COOKING WITH SALT

Salt's purpose, like a fork, is multipronged. First and foremost, it is meant to enhance flavor. When used properly, it should not make food taste salty, but rather bring out the natural essence of the food. But historically salt's importance centered on its preservative capability. Salt leaches water out of foods, eliminating the hospitable moist environment needed for the growth of mold and bacteria. It is not only the drying that is important, though. A salty environment also prevents the survival of pathogenic organisms. This was, as you can imagine, key in the pre-fridge era.

But today, with our ultrafood consciousness, salt is being added as its own ingredient. Smoky salts, salts infused with clay or charcoal, herby and spicy salts, salt with extra umami or a hint of sugar are being added to layer more flavor, and not simply to enhance the flavors already there. And it is not just the tongue that gets to partake. Colorful salts add visual interest to dishes, and varying textures are adding crunch. Not only does your salad get a burst of flavor, but it looks different, and has a new mouthfeel. As you will find in the recipe chapters to come, salt is now a featured player.

HOW SALTS DIFFER

Just as beef tastes different in Oklahoma, Japan, and Argentina, so, too, varies the flavor of salt.

The difference in climate, soil, mineral deposits, flora, and fauna vary both on land and sea, and all impart specific flavors to salt.

In general, salt that is harvested from inland deposits is saltier than sea salt. It is also harder, which makes sense if you think about it being compressed under layers of dinosaurs for millennia. Sea salt is almost fluffy in comparison. Of course, these facts vary, too. For instance, Murray River salt from Australia is extracted through natural brine from prehistoric sediments, but their evaporation process makes it one of the lightest, fluffiest salts on the market.

Another general, though not universal, rule is that sea salt has more flavor. These salts still have residual sea stuck to them, so, of course, they are more complex. That said, there are some pretty boring sea salts. These generalizations are not really that helpful, though, because there are exceptions. But keep reading! There is only one surefire way to know which salts you like, and that is to try them. So continue your salt journey, and be sure to experience "A Salt Tasting" on page 25.

A MARKET GUIDE TO ARTISAN SALT, AND A SALT TASTING

BASIC SALT TERMINOLOGY
INTERNATIONAL ARTISAN SALTS
A SALT TASTING

T his chapter is designed to acquaint you with the artisan salts of the world. The examples listed are the ones you can most easily find in stores and online. It is by no means a comprehensive list. Such a thing would be difficult because new saltworks pop up every year as more chefs discover the importance of good salt. Here you can familiarize yourself with salt production around the world, and the various attributes that make each salt unique. Some of these saltworks are well-known, and have been awarded special *terroir* status. Some are historically significant. Some are run by interesting people who use interesting techniques. Some are just weird. I consider all these criteria when choosing a salt. You will, no doubt, discover more salt in your travels than are on this list. (I always do.)

The most important criterion, though, for choosing a salt, is the taste. For that reason, after the guide there is a step-by-step outline for a salt tasting. This is the very best way for you to figure out which of these zillion salts you like and want to cook with.

basic salt terminology

BLOCK SALT/SALT BLOCK. This is usually a reference to large blocks of Himalayan or Bolivian salt, cut into slabs for use in cooking or serving (see pages 84 and 159). There are other salts cut into slabs, but these pink mountain salts are the most common.

CITRIC SALT. This is another name for citric acid, the thing that makes your Sour Patch Kids puckery. It is not really a salt, but I do use it from time to time to sour things up. It is available in gourmet markets.

CURING SALT. This is a reference to sodium nitrate, or saltpeter. It is fairly toxic, and not meant for general cooking—just for curing meats. See the sidebar on page 60.

FLAKE SALT. This is a general category of salt that refers to a particular crystalline form, known as a lamellose structure, or lamella. This occurs when there is a different growth rate between the face and the edges of the crystals. Depending on the atmospheric conditions, and the evaporation methods used by a saltworks, shapes will vary from pyramids to boxes to sheets. Flake salt generally has a lower mineral content, which means a saltier taste. Their thin, flat shape makes them crunchy and quick to dissolve, which is perfect for finishing. Flake salts are produced all over the world.

FLOWER OF THE SEA. These salts are solar evaporated and hand harvested. Crystals form on the top of open pools and are raked off daily during the harvest. These salts are lower in sodium, dissolve quickly, and tend to be flaky and delicate.

FOSSIL SALT/MARINE FOSSIL SALT. Terms that refer to ancient salts mined from mountain interiors, such as Himalayan and Bolivian.

GREY SALT. This is English for *sel gris*, the salt that sinks to the bottom of the ponds after fleur de sel has been removed. It is still really good.

HALITE. This is the scientific name for rock salt, which has the chemical composition NaCL—sodium chloride.

KOSHER SALT. This is not a salt that is kosher, but a salt designed for koshering. Its larger grain is necessary in the kosher butchering process. It removes surface blood by desiccation, the same process used for curing meat. The animal is covered in salt and left for an hour or so. During that time the salt absorbs the body fluids, and is then rinsed away. Kosher salt has been a mainstay for chefs because it has no additives, and its flat plate shape, made by pressing cubic crystals between rollers, dissolves quickly and is easy to pinch. Lately, though, thanks to the artisanal salt movement, there has been a backlash against kosher salt in favor of traditional sea salts. I admit that, although I am a huge fan of good-quality sea salt, I was trained to use kosher, and old habits die hard. It does not offend my palate as much as some chefs purport. But, at the same time, it does not excite my palate either.

MOUNTAIN SALT. This is a generic term used to describe salt that is mined from a mountain. It is a little confusing because the same salts are simultaneously described as sea salt (they were, after all, once part of a sea), rock salt, fossil salt, or marine fossil salt, which makes them sound as far away from a mountain as you can get. It is a vast category, with many completely unique examples.

ROCK SALT. There are two definitions for rock salt:

1. A salt that is mined from the earth (i.e., from rocks) in large slabs or chunks. This is also called mountain salt, fossil salt, and fossil marine salt.

2. Large chunks of salt that are meant for consumption. It is still used in cooking to chill the ice in your ice cream machine, or to nestle your oysters in (see page 150). It is also used to de-ice your street.

SEA SALT. This is a generic term for salt that is made by evaporating seawater. Salt, mined from mountains containing ancient sea beds, is sometimes referred to as sea salt, but I think that is just confusing. By that logic, you need to call all salt sea salt. But we don't do that, because we need some parameters.

UNREFINED SALT. Salt in its natural form is unrefined. Man has not altered it. Unrefined sea salt has more flavor, more texture, and at least eighty different natural minerals and elements. By contrast, refined salt has two elements—sodium and chloride. All the salts recommended in this book are unrefined. This includes both the rock and sea salts. Recipes for infused salts call for an unrefined sea salt, which is to say, any good-quality, unprocessed, natural sea salt.

international artisan salts

ALAEA. (Hawaii). This red sea salt has traditionally been made by bringing water from tidal pools into evaporating pans that have been dug out of the sacred volcanic baked red clay called alaea. The clay is red from a high level of iron oxide. The salt made with it had both spiritual and medicinal uses. Today it is known mainly for its inclusion in traditional Hawaiian dishes (see Kahlúa Pig on page 144, Tuna Poke on page 153, and Pipikaula on page 73). Unfortunately, most of the "Hawaiian Salt" that you find is actually mass-produced in California. For the authentic stuff, look for specific place names, like Haleakala, or Molokai.

ALASKAN ALDER. *See Smoked Salts.*

AMERICAN SEA SALTS. (Various Regions). Saint Andrew's Bay, on the panhandle of Florida, is a deep estuary with a high salinity due to low freshwater inflow. Here, a number of saltworks grew in importance during the Civil War, when salt was extremely important, not only for food preservation but also to a busy leather tanning industry. The destruction of the saltworks by Union troops was vital to the defeat of the Confederacy. Here, a Panama City culinary instructor started classic salt production as a school fundraiser. Now, Gulf Coast Saltworks is available to us.

In Charleston, South Carolina, Bulls Bay Salt Works is harnessing the healthy saltwater ecosystem in the Cape Romain National Wildlife Refuge. They pump water from Bulls Bay into greenhouses that utilize the sun and wind for evaporation.

The Pacific Northwest has a long history of salt making. (Don't get me started on Lewis and Clark again—love those guys.) San Juan Island Sea Salt uses mostly solar energy to reduce water from the south end of San Juan Island in Puget Sound. After the water concentrates to a brine in greenhouses, electricity gently heats the brine in the final stages to create the small, delicate flakes.

Cold, Arctic water from the Gulf of Maine is gathered at Buck's Harbor, then pumped into a series of greenhouses. There the wind is allowed to blow through, and it combines with the heat from the sun to concentrate, then evaporate, the shallow pools. The simple, natural technique used at the Maine Sea Salt Company is historically connected to the region, a fact that they are rightly proud of.

ANDES ROSE (Bolivia). Also called Bolivian Pink and Bolivian Rose, this rock salt comes from the Andes Mountain range. It is salt from an ancient sea, deposited 3 million years ago and protected from the elements and pollution. Its color ranges from very light to very dark pink from various levels of iron oxide. It can be bought in various textures, as well as chunks and blocks.

ANGLESEY (Wales, UK). Sea salt has been produced on this island since the eighteenth century. Today the Halen Môn company produces a highly sought after soft, flaky salt from their saltworks situated on the Menai Strait. Because the water of the strait flows in swift currents,

and is filtered through the sand, it is considered very pure. (The founders, who began as aquarium operators, claim the water is so pure that sea horses—notoriously finicky about where they get it on—will breed in it.) The company was recently granted protected status with the European Union, which recognizes foods produced in a specific region with specific expertise. The salt is available smoked and infused.

ARABIAN FLEUR DE SEL (Pakistan). Harvested from the Arabian Sea (not necessarily by Arabian salt makers), it is so named because it evaporated in solar pools and is hand raked like the French fleur de sel. But this salt more closely resembles a jumbo version of Bali Pyramid. In the hot, windy desert the water evaporates quickly to form large pyramid crystals that are crunchy but light.

ATLAS SALT (Morocco). At the base of the Atlas Mountains in Southwest Morocco there is a village called Mellha. If you travel by foot (or donkey) into the foothills you will find an ancient mellau albir (salt spring) dug hundreds of years ago. Water is pulled up in buckets by hand and left to evaporate in pools. The resulting salt is packed back down to the village. Also called Moroccan Spring Salt and the Tears of Atlas, it is a pinkish white salt with fairly large crystals, a mild flavor for a rock salt, and a crumbly texture. It reminds me of Murray River, with a little more weight. I prefer this salt to Moroccan Atlantic when making North African dishes.

BALI PYRAMID. *See Indonesian Salt.*

BAVARIAN SALT (Austria/Germany). Salt from these mountains has been mined since people first settled in the region. Most of what is left must now be extracted through solution mining (the injection of water followed then by evaporation) rather than pickaxes. This salt, which can vary in color from white to sandy and speckled, is fantastic for general use. There are many mines in the region, most of which have tours, and which you absolutely must visit.

BAMBOO SALT (Korea). Traditional bamboo salt refers to a technique that originated in Korea, and which produces a special salt, known as *jook yeom*. A hollow piece of bamboo is packed with sea salt, its ends are capped with yellow clay, and the bamboo is roasted in a kiln. It is thought to have medicinal and cosmetic benefits. The same technique can be found elsewhere in Asia, but beware of the imposters. Some salts are simply tinted green and infused with bamboo leaf extract. You'll be able to tell the difference, because while the imitation salt is pastel green and tastes a bit grassy, the real thing is a dark purple-brown and tastes very strongly of smoke, sulphur, and minerals.

BLACK DIAMOND. This is the black version of Cyprus Pyramid salt. As with other black salts (like Black Lava) it is infused with charcoal, and is thought to have detoxifying benefits. It is different than the Hawaiian version, though. Black Diamond consists of huge pyramidal crystals that are very crunchy, yet dissolve quickly. The flavor is milder than its white counterpart, which makes it suitable for more applications.

BLACK LAVA. This sea salt has been infused with activated charcoal during the final stages of drying, which turns the salt jet-black. It has a surprisingly mild flavor, and is believed to have detoxifying properties. The most important property to me is visual—it looks amazing sprinkled across contrasting colored foods. As with alaea, there are imitation black Hawaiian salts, and it's best to look for place names, such as Kilauea.

BLACK SALT. *See Kala Namak.*

BRAZILIAN SAL GROSSO. Solar-evaporated sea salt from the Atlantic Ocean, it is fairly strong, and more suited to general cooking than finishing, unless it is to top off very strong flavors.

CARIBBEAN SEA SALT (Cayman Islands). The story of this salt is a lesson in ingenuity. Coastal real estate prices precluded the development of evaporation ponds. But after Hurricane Ivan in 2004, the Cayman Sea Salt company opened up shop in an effort to help revitalize the devastated community. Water is brought from the pollution-free western Caribbean, brine is concentrated in large tanks, then transferred to evaporation tables that are constructed out of glass discarded after the hurricane. Nice, huh? The other noteworthy salt operation in the Caribbean is Cargill's plant on the island of Bonaire. The salt made there is sent to the States for industrial processing, and is only worth mentioning because it is a huge farm. I understand that the white salt mountains can be seen from your Caribbean cruise lido deck.

CELTIC SEA SALT (France). *See also Fleur de Sel, Sel gris.* The French believe that it was the Celts that first harvested salt in Brittany, the region now famous for salt making, long before the Romans arrived. However, just because the label says Celtic does not mean it is hand harvested or of good quality. But even a cheap Celtic salt can be useful for applications that use a ton of salt, like whole salted fish (see page 156). If you want the good stuff, look for Fleur de sel or Sel gris on the label.

CORNISH SEA SALT (Cornwall, UK). Salt has been produced along the south coast of Cornwall since the Iron Age. We know this because, like Essex, Cornwall contains remnants of *briquetage* vessels—red clay pots used by ancient salt makers to reduce their seawater. The climate is not conducive to solar evaporation here. Instead, filtered seawater is heated in vats, and the resulting pure flakes are hand harvested.

CYPRUS BLACK. *See Black Diamond.*

CYPRUS SEA SALT. Thanks to two salt lakes, Lanarca and Limassol, Cyprus was a major salt exporter from the Middle Ages until the 1980s. Tons of salt was harvested from the lake beds when they dried up in the summer months. Then an airport was built just prior to World War II, and the island became an important hub for travel from the Middle East to Europe. When the airport was expanded, construction drastically reduced the quality of the salt, and much of the lake bed has now become a long-term parking lot. Luckily, salt does still come from Cyprus. Today, seawater is pumped into one of several industrial facilities, and

through solar evaporation is gradually heated over a two-year period to create the trademark pyramidal crystals. The pyramids, also referred to as Cyprus Flake, or Cyprus Pyramid, have a great texture, but can sometimes be overly salty. Try out the different manufacturers to find the one that suits you best.

DEAD SEA SALT (Israel, Jordan, Syria, Lebanon, Palestine, Egypt). This salt is used mainly for therapeutic products, including bath salts and body scrubs. It has a relatively small amount of sodium chloride—only about 15 percent as opposed to other sea salts that typically contain above 80 percent, and table salt, which has about 97 percent. The high level of magnesium it contains is considered beneficial to osteoarthritis and skin ailments, but is unsuitable for culinary use. I have, nevertheless, seen stores selling Dead Sea salt that is meant for cooking. The quality is not noteworthy.

FIORE DI SALE (Italy). *Fiore di sale* is Italy's version of "flower of the sea." Evaporated by the sun and hand harvested on warm windless mornings, it comes from either the Adriatic coast (see Il Sale dei Papi) or from the area of Sicily known as the salt road, stretching along the coast from Trapani to Marsala. Both locations have the perfect combination of Mediterranean temperature, wind, and low rainfall. Saltwork technology was thought to have been started in these locations by the Phoenicians. Old windmills, dating from at least 800 AD, are still used to pump water into grinding mills, and modern mills have been built to 1500 AD Turkish specifications. There are salt museums all along the salt road that you can visit. Until recently, the Italian government held a monopoly on salt production, and all the salt produced was shipped to a government facility for packaging. Now that the regulations have been lifted, local salt producers are reclaiming their trade. These salt flakes, like other flowers of the sea, come in medium-large crystals, are lower in sodium, and dissolve easily, making them great for finishing and table salting.

FLEUR DE SEL DE GUÉRANDE (France). This is the French "flower of the sea," collected off the coast of Brittany. Seawater is channeled from the Atlantic ocean, via canals, into shallow marshes where it is left to evaporate. As salt crystals begin to form on the surface of the ponds, they are raked off by hand with traditional wooden tools. (Much is made of the wooden rakes, called *lousse à fleur*.) Because the aquatic environment varies from year to year, the salt does, too. It is certainly the most well-known of the artisan salts, and was the first to get worldwide recognition. It is also, in my opinion, the snootiest of salts. (If a salt can be such a thing.) The French credit the Celts for instituting this process 1,000 years ago. But there are those who contend it might have been Vikings, who came in search of a reliable salt source so that they could enter the salt cod trade. Either way, it's old. But the same methods are used all over the world, with similar wooden tools, with just as much reverence and tradition. All I'm saying is, it is not necessarily the best.

FLOR BLANCA. *See Manzanillo.*

FLOR DE SAL (Spain and Portugal). These are two versions of solar-evaporated, hand-harvested flower-of-the-sea salts, also referred to as the Spanish and Portuguese fleur de sel. In Spain it is produced in several spots—southern Cadiz, eastern Ebro Delta in Catalonia, and on the islands of Ibiza and Mallorca. These locations and traditional methods were first used by the Romans. In Portugal the finest sea salts come from the Algarve, which is the southernmost coastal region along the Atlantic. Harvest occurs during the summer months, when, every day, only the uppermost crystals are raked by hand off the top of the evaporation ponds. They are dried in the sun, with no bleaching, no additives, and no mechanical processes of any kind.

GUAVA. *See Smoked Salt.*

HAKANAI FLAKE. *See Japanese Shio.*

HALEN MÔN. *See Anglesey.*

HANA FLAKE. *See Japanese Shio.*

HAWAIIAN SALT. Usually the term *Hawaiian salt* refers to the red alaea. But there are several artisan salts made in Hawaii in the traditional manner, and kept white. Many are harvested to be turned into the black or red salt, but they can still be had in their pure form. Look for traditional names like Kona, Pa'akai, or Papohaku.

HIMALAYAN PINK (Pakistan). This salt from the mountains of northern Pakistan is a mined marine fossil salt. Estimated to be over 250 million years old, this salt was formed from an ancient sea, dehydrated and buried by shifting tectonic plates. The modern mine tunnels a half mile into the mountain range, and spans over 40 square miles. Because it has been buried for so long, it is considered some of the purest salt on earth. The color ranges from white to deep pink, and it comes in various textures and forms, including blocks.

HIWA KAI. *See Black Lava.*

IL SALE DEI PAPI (Italy). From Cervia, on Italy's Adriatic coast, this flower of the sea is noteworthy because the first harvest of the year goes directly onto the papal table. The two producers of note are Salina Camillone and Salfiore de Romagna.

INCAN SUN SALT. *See Maras.*

INDIAN BLACK SALT. *See Kala Namak.*

INDONESIAN SALT (Java). Salt has been produced in this region for hundreds of years. In Bali, along the eastern coastline, the Strait of Lombok contains both cool water from the north and warmer water from the south. Combined with tropical winds, this region facilitates an amazingly textured pyramid salt. Here, hundreds of small salt farmers practice traditional methods of solar evaporation and hand harvesting. Products include Bali Pyramid, Balinese fleur de sel, *Bali kechil* (which means "small" or "baby"), *Bali rama* (which means "big" or "daddy"). There is salt production elsewhere in Indonesia, too, including the Madura Island, northeast of Java. The area was historically exploited by the Dutch to supply their territories in the region.

JURASSIC SEA SALT (Utah). This sweet, bright salt has specks of brown and pink and tan that come from upwards of 60 trace minerals. It comes from an ancient seabed in central Utah that was sealed from the elements (and pollutants) by a volcanic eruption. When this salt is ground fine it looks just like the sand in a Utah desert. There are also Jurassic salts mined from the salt domes along the Gulf Coast of Texas.

JAPANESE SHIO (Japan). The Japanese have perhaps the most diverse range of artisan salts (or *shio*) on the planet.

Salt making has a history hundreds of years old, but for much of the twentieth century those traditions were lost. Salt production came under strict governmental control to ensure steady supply. This monopoly greatly reduced artisanal production in favor of large industrial facilities. When the restrictions were lifted in 1997, local saltworks slowly made their way back.

Some of the salt-making techniques are pretty standard—concentrating seawater, and then drying it over a heat source. But there are also saltworks that utilize much more intricate processes.

Region is an important factor in the quality of shio. And because Japan does not have a particularly hot climate, the saltworks here utilize a variety of unique evaporation methods.

• *Aguni no Shio* is reduced by repeatedly spraying water onto bamboo stalks and letting it trickle down, while simultaneously being exposed to the wind.

• *Suzu shio* is similarly evaporated by trickling down bamboo mats.

• *Temomi Tenpien Enmusubi* is evaporated by

sun, wind, and by flowing down layers of cloth. But here, after crystallization, the salt is hand kneaded daily for a month.

• Salt made in the *Agehama* style carries seawater by bucket to a flat sand terrace. It is left for 100 days on sand, during which time the water become superconcentrated. The sand is collected, the salt washed from it with more seawater that is then boiled away over a carefully controlled wood fire.

• *Yukishio snow salt* is made from water brought from a coral reef area off the Miyako Island in the Okinawa prefecture. This fine, dusty powdered salt is considered to have the world's highest mineral content.

• *Moshio* is salt infused with the essence of seaweed. This traditional method begins by drying seaweed in the sun, then collecting the accumulated salt crystals, now rich in umami.

• *Hana No Shio (Hana Flake)* and *Hakanai Flake* are delicate hand-harvested flake salts. The Noto Peninsula is considered to have saltier, cleaner water. Salt production began here at least 500 years ago because this area is not suitable for agriculture. During the Edo period the local ruling clan initiated a rice-for-salt system, wherein those without adequate land borrowed rice from the government and paid for it in salt at a fixed rate.

• *Nazuna* is a particularly briny sea salt.

• *Moon salt* is made from water that is harvested in the full moon light, which is believed to yield a higher mineral content, and the energy of the full moon.

• *Takesumi Bamboo Deep Sea* is made in the same manner as Korean *jook yeom* (See Bamboo Salt on page 15).

There are many more Japanese artisanal salts (upwards of 1,500 producers today), using both traditional and modern methods. Keeping up with modern demand, there are even salts that are infused and smoked. The best thing to do, as a salt connoisseur, is to work your way through them, making notes and experimenting.

KALA NAMAK (India). Used extensively in Indian and Ayurvedic cuisines, as well as spiritual purification, blessing, and healing rituals, this weird-looking salt has a strong sulfuric aroma, like hard-boiled eggs. Salt is harvested from Himalayan ranges, sealed in ceramic jars with charcoal, traditional aromatic seeds and spices (notably the *harad* seed from the black Myrobalan tree), fired at high temperature for twenty-four hours, and then aged. The result is a change in the chemical composition, transforming the sodium sulfate into hydrogen sulfide and sodium sulfide. This produces the coveted sulfuric properties, especially appreciated by vegans, who like its egg-like flavors. It is often referred to as black salt, but it is actually a deep purple-brown, and looks more pink when ground fine. It can be bought in large rocks or ground to various degrees. (See Jal Jeera, page 192, Khara Lassi Granita, page 197, and Raita, page 137).

KIMCHI SALT. *See Sogum.*

KOREAN SEA SALT. *See Sogum.*

LÆSØE SALT (Denmark). Scandinavia had a real salt problem in the Middle Ages. The northern climate precluded the warm and windy coastlines needed for natural salt evaporation. But on Læsøe Island, in the middle of the North Sea bay of Kattegat, there is a salt marsh with naturally concentrated water. There, salt manufacturers set up shop, using wood to generate heat for evaporation, until the forests were completely stripped. The operation was shut down by the Danish crown in the sixteenth century and the salt operation was moved to Iceland. There are no trees to provide fuel in Iceland, but there is plenty of geothermal activity. (See Saltverk, page 23.) Today Læsøe produces a small amount of salt, using sustainable methods, mostly for historic tourism.

LAKE ASSAL (Djibouti). From one of the saltiest bodies of water on earth comes a naturally occurring spherical salt. It can be as large as a grapefruit or as small as fine pearls. There are other spherical salts that are made by artificially tumbling large salt crystals. But here, the supersaturation of the water combined with the heat, wind, and waves does it naturally. The larger balls must be grated, which, in my opinion, robs them of the fascination. The smaller pearls are easier, and more interesting, if a little clunky. Vietnamese Pearl salt is a completely different thing—not at all spherical, but rather irregular, coarse, very hard lumps.

MALDON (Essex, UK). Salt has been made in Essex since well before the Romans arrived in 300 BC. We know this because archeologists have identified historic salt-making sites by the red mounds of earth (a.k.a. the red hills of Essex). These mounds were formed by layers of debris that included red clay vessels called *briquetage* used to evaporate seawater during the Iron Age. The Maldon company is the only salt producer

in the area now, established in the late 1800s. Situated at the head of the Blackwater Estuary, water is gathered only during spring tides, when it is at its saltiest. (The flat marshes and low rainfall during that time of year means high salinity.) That water is held in tanks for processing throughout the year. The water is then filtered and boiled slowly to produce the wide pyramidal flakes coveted by the world's chefs. Indeed, this is one of the first salts I fell in love with. It works across the board, and is beautiful.

MALI SALT (Sahara). Up until the end of the sixteenth century, salt from the Sahara Desert was the most important commodity of the region, and resulted in the rise of Empires (the Songhai, Ghana, and Mali), and the spread of Islam. Caravans, with each camel carrying hundreds of pounds of salt slabs strapped to its humps, transported salt across the continent, creating the earliest trade networks. Salt, so plentiful in the Sahara, was virtually unattainable in the savanna and the interior forests. It was exchanged for food from other regions, slaves, ivory, horses, and gold (which, in some cases was traded pound for pound). Timbuktu, once an ancient hub of scholarship and trade five times the size of London, is now virtually abandoned. But caravans still carry salt slabs from the ancient lakebeds—some by camel, some by truck—to the remnants of this city, now 1/200 the size of London. The salt is used for local culinary and industrial consumption, and is exported to us. The very idea of consuming such an ancient treasure gives me goose bumps.

MANZANILLO, FLOR DE SAL (Mexico). A Mexican solar-evaporated hand-harvested flower of the sea, also referred to as Mexican fleur de sel. In the Mexican state of Colima, *salineros* at the Lagoon de Cuyutlán have continuously produced salt in the same manner as was used when the area was ruled by the Tarascans in the sixteenth century. As with most salts produced in this manner, it is delicate and flaky.

MARAS, SAL DE (Peru). This pink-hued salt has been extracted from underground saline springs of the Andes since the time of the Incas. The spring is nestled in the Sacred Valley of the Incas, between Cuzco and Macho Picchu. Water trickles through channels into thousands of terraced pools. (I highly recommend a Google image search—it is impressive.) Because the site is far away from civilization, there is little pollution, adding to the purity of this salt. It is also called Peruvian Pink and Incan Sun Salt.

MAYAN SALT (El Salvador). This is the Mayan version of flower of the sea, produced today in coastal El Salvador using traditional Mayan methods. Clean water is captured in mangrove forest evaporation pools lined with volcanic soil. The resulting salt has a high mineral content and mild ocean-y flavor. The Mayans had a vast salt trading network, throughout what is now Guatemala, El Salvador, Belize, Honduras, and the Yucatan. Historians believe that several tons of salt were moved each day, by boat and by foot, into the interior Mayan territories.

MAYAN SUN. *See Mayan Salt.*

MOON SALT *See Japanese Shio.*

MOROCCAN ATLANTIC (Morocco). Moroccan sea salt is produced on the flats near Oualida, south of Casablanca on the west coast of Africa. Atlantic ocean water is pumped into open salt pans and left to evaporate over a period of months. It is a fine general-purpose salt, but it appears far more in health and beauty products than it does in recipes.

MUOI BIEN (Vietnam). Vietnam has a long history of salt farming, and plenty of coastlines to use. Their product is evaporated in the sun and hand raked. The crystals are big, pure, and mineral rich. Unfortunately much of the salt produced this year (2015) was thrown back into the sea, while the government imported 150,000 tons of industrial salt from China. There is concern that this practice will not only cause financial hardship for the farmers, but also mineral deficiencies in the population. If you can find some of this great salt, buy it. The artisans could use your support.

MURRAY RIVER SALT (Australia). This salt comes from an underground spring in New South Wales. Water flows down from the Australian Alps into the Murray-Darling Basin, where low rainfall and high heat combine to concentrate the groundwater into an underground brine. Water is pumped and channeled into solar evaporation pools, where it sits throughout the summer before crystals are washed and dried. It has an apricot color that comes from a specific carotene-rich, salt-tolerant river algae. Extremely light and fluffy, it dissolves fast but still has a nice crunch.

PANGASINAN STAR (Philippines). Salt is still hand harvested in the traditional manner at the north end of the Philippines' largest island, Luzon. In the Pangasinan province (a name that means, essentially, "Land of Salt") the salt season begins when the rainy season ends, from December to May, when the weather is dry, and daily temperatures hover around 100°F. The clear water of the South China Sea evaporates fast here, creating a unique crystal structure that is both grainy and flaky.

PEARL SALT. *See Lake Assal.*

PERUVIAN PINK. *See Maras.*

PERSIAN BLUE (Iran). This crazy rock salt comes from salt mines of Semman, in northern Iran. Within a more common pink salt formation runs a vein that has become blue through high compression. (The process, as I understand it, is similar to that of blue glacier ice.) The crystals are chunky and hard, with flecks of blue. (When ground fine it looks white, which is much less exciting.) The flavor is strong—almost sulfuric initially—and a little tingly. But it softens after a bit.

PHETCHABURI SEA SALT (Thailand). Because this land is too salty to grow rice, the bulk of Thailand's salt is produced along the coast in the provinces of Samut Sakhon, Samut Songkhram, and Phetchaburi. This region was, in earlier centuries, a major stop on trade routes from China and India. Today, when you drive south from Bangkok along Highway 35 you will be surrounded by salt pans and windmills, pumping in water from the Gulf of Thailand. Between October and April, it takes only about a week for the sun to evaporate the

water, and for the salt to reach raking stage. There is not much export, but the region has recently been promoting its salt industry as a tourist attraction, and in Petchaburi they have begun an annual Salt Festival. Like other salty bodies of water around the world, this shoreline attracts an amazing variety of waterfowl, and is considered the best spot for bird-watching in Thailand.

PIRAN SALT (Slovenia). Salt has been in production on the northeastern shore of the Adriatic since the thirteenth century. Control of the site has shifted periodically. The Venetian Republic was in charge between the fifteenth and eighteenth centuries. Austria had it after that. When Yugoslavia got it after World War I, they instituted industrial salt facilities. Then in 1989 the city of Piran established Sečovlje Salina Nature Park. Now the Republic of Slovenia protects this salt pond ecosystem. Salt is a big deal here, and has earned EU-protected designation. They even gave it a festival, marking the beginning of salt season in April. This saltwork insists the secret to its success is an artificial *petola*, a crust formation of green algae, gypsum, carbonate minerals, and clay. It acts as a biological filter and prevents the mixing of salt with the sea mud at the bottoms of ponds.

POTASSIUM NITRATE. *See Curing Salt.*

RED SEA SALT (Eritrea). Salt pans were established along the Eastern coast of Africa by Italian colonists in the early twentieth century. The Red Sea has very high salinity, and a water temperature of around 80°F. As a result, along the Eritrean Coast, there is a wide variety of unique aquatic life and a particularly healthy coral reef. The salt harvested there has a coral quality—briny, chunky, hard—but is rather beautiful in its irregularity.

SAHARA DESERT SALT. *See Mali Salt.*

SALTVERK (Iceland). Salt was first made in Iceland in the seventeenth century by the Danes. Because there is no lumber in Iceland, salt makers turned to the geothermal heat of the geysers. This practice was recently reestablished using traditional methods. Clean seawater is pumped into open evaporation pans heated by geysers. They produce a black charcoal-infused salt, a salt smoked over birch wood, as well as a number of flavor infusions.

SANCHAL. *See Kala Namak.*

SEL GRIS. This term generally refers to grey sea salt from France, but it is used generically to reference salts made with the same method around the world. Grey salt is the solar-evaporated, hand-harvested salt that is the residual, leftover, backwash of salt after the fleur de sel (flower or salt) has been harvested. If that description made sel gris sound bad, let me assure you that I love it! This was the first artisan salt I ever tried. It was given to me as a gift by chef Jacques Chauvet when we both worked for Le Cordon Bleu schools. He was trying to make me more French, and it totally worked. Sel gris comes from a number of saltworks, in a number of grinds—from coarse to "velvet." It is also cheaper than most artisan salts, so you can make it your everyday go-to. (Although, I can never settle on just one everyday go-to.)

SMOKED SALT. There are many smoked salts on the market, and just about every artisan saltwork offers their product in a smoked form. The wood chosen for smoking is determined by region. In Scandinavia salt is smoked over birch and juniper (which is sometimes called Viking Salt). In Alaska they use alder. In Hawaii they use wood from the guava tree. Halen Môn is smoked over oak. Throughout the Northwest you can find hickory, apple wood, and mesquite being used. It is safe to say that if you are in the market for smoked salt, it won't take long to find one you like. Or, you can easily make your own (see page 50).

SOGUM (Korea). This salt, also known as Korean Sea Salt or Kimchi Salt, comes from Shineui Island off the west coast of South Korea. It is solar evaporated and hand harvested from pools that UNESCO has recognized as extra-clean and extra-biodiverse. This salt is unusual in that it is aged for up to three years in wood, giving the chunky crystals a smoother taste.

TIBETAN ROSE SEA SALT. *See Himalayan.*

TIMBUKTU SALT. *See Mali Salt.*

VIKING SALT. *See Smoked Salt.*

a salt tasting

Now it's time to figure out which of these salts you like, and what to do with them.

One of the many jobs I have held in the culinary industry is instructor. And my favorite work as an instructor happens with the US Navy, where I am periodically asked to train galley cooks. It's a job that has taken me all over the world, visiting many ships and naval bases. And every time I go, I bring salt—and I make the salty dogs eat it.

Most of the galley cooks (known today by the enlisted rating of Culinary Specialists, or CS) receive limited training in the kitchen, and even less culinary exposure. They are also all pretty young. So, with a few exceptions, they are not the greatest cooks, nor do they have much of a culinary frame of reference. Yet they are responsible for feeding what can be, if they serve on a carrier, as many as 7,000 sailors. My job is to make them better at their jobs.

I discovered that by having them taste a number of different salts, each with very different characteristics, and comparing them to the table salt the Navy procures, the CSs began to understand how their palates work. Suddenly, they could see just how different food can taste, and how much variation their tongues could detect. Not to brag, but I credit my galley salt tastings with turning a fair number of CSs into great cooks.

Now it's your turn.

There are no real rules to a salt tasting, but I have some suggestions.

• CHOOSE YOUR SALT

The beginning of this chapter has a substantial list to get you started. I find it best to limit your tasting to five to six salts in the beginning. If you try too many at first, the process becomes overwhelming. Save the next five for another day. (Something to look forward to!)

You can choose your salt based on specific criteria, like salts from a specific region or country, salts that are made using the same technique, or made by using completely different techniques. You can gather a completely random assortment, or purchase a starter kit from a salt purveyor.

• PRESENT YOUR SALT

Serve your salt in tiny dishes, and provide tiny spoons to scoop it with. (No one wants to eat salt that was touched by the guy in front of them in the buffet line.) Line them up, arranged from mild to strong. This may be harder with some assortments, but in general, save rock and smoked salts for the finish. I also like to finish, if I can, with a generic table salt, just to drive the point home.

Make labels for your salts. Include the name of the salt, the region it comes from, the style of salt it is (sea salt, mined rock salt, etc.), and anything else you think is interesting. There are some proponents of the blind salt tasting, but I am not one of them.

• PREPARE TASTING FOODS

Now comes the fun part! Prepare foods for your guests to sprinkle with salt. The examples below are listed in order of importance. (In other words, if you're on a budget, just get bread and butter—it will still provide amazing insight.)

—French bread smeared with unsalted butter
—Grilled beef (rare to medium rare)
—Cucumbers
—Plain boiled potatoes
—Seasonal fruit (try melon, a mild tropical like mango, or strawberries—nothing too acidic)
—Dark chocolate
—Caramel of some sort: candies or sauce
—Mild cheese: chèvre or a triple crème like St. Andre
—Radishes
—Tomatoes
—Milk and white chocolate
—Chocolate chip cookies
—Macaroni and cheese, Fettuccine Alfredo, or something with a similar creamy sauce
—Ice Cream: vanilla or chocolate
—Chicken or duck
—Shrimp

Prepare these foods (cooked when necessary) in bite-size pieces. I like to provide enough pieces of food that every person can taste each salt with each food. So, for instance, if I was having five guests, and I was featuring five salts, I would prepare twenty-five small slices of buttered bread. In the case of ice cream, nestle the container in a bowl of ice and rock salt to keep it cold, provide small cups or cones, and an ice cream scoop nearby in a glass of water. When your guests arrive, explain how they should proceed. Take a plate of food, sprinkle on the salts, and experience their unique qualities side by side.

If you can, offer your guests a tasting note sheet. (See the sample on the facing page.) It will be easy to forget which was which, and which went better with what. Plus, with a sheet of impressions to take home, everyone will be more likely to try these salts in their own kitchens.

And don't forget the water. Lots of water.

sample salt tasting table

Here is an example of a table you can use during your tasting. There are no right or wrong answers, because taste in food, like taste in art, is subjective. I consider cooking art, so, if it helps, think of this exercise as choosing, then mixing your colors..

SALT	STEAK	CUCUMBER	BREAD/BUTTER	CHOCOLATE	MISC. NOTES
MALDON (Essex, UK)	Nice balance w/ umami and texture	Brought out veg taste a lot	Nice crunch. Saltier finish	Nice, but stronger saltiness than Atlas	Stronger than I expected
BLACK DIAMOND (Cyprus)	A bit too chunky	Crunchy, mild, refreshing. Great look	Loved the look and texture	Great combo— but can't really see it	Very crunchy, milder. Looks so cool
ATLAS MOUNTAIN (Morocco)	Perfect balance. Slightly crunchy for a minute	So subtle, and mineral-y	Crunch, milder than Maldon. Nice salty aftertaste	Great crunch— good look. Best flavor in aftertaste	This is my favorite finish
SAN JUAN ISLAND (USA)	Really nice, dissolves best	Very nice, but no wow factor	Pronounced sea flavor	Less crunch. A little too salty	Would be a good everyday salt
VIKING SALT (Denmark)	Amazing	No thanks	Liked it better on meat than bread	Very interesting finish	Best for meat, but sweet was so fun

PART 2

COOKING WITH SALT

MAKING INFUSED SALTS

AGAVE SALT
ANCHOVY SALT
ANISE SALT
ASH SALT
BACON SALT
BOURBON SALT
CAPER SALT
CELERY SALT
CHIPOTLE SALT
CHOCOLATE SALT
CITRUS SALT
CURRY SALT
DASHI SALT
DATE SALT
DRIED HERB AND
    SPICE SALT

ESPRESSO SALT
FLOWER SALT
FRESH HERB SALT
GARLIC SALT
GINGER SALT
GRAND MARNIER SALT
HOJICHA SALT
HORSERADISH SALT
KALE SALT
LI HIN MUI SALT
MAPLE SALT
MATCHA SALT
MUSTARD SALT
NUT SALT
OLIVE SALT

ONION SALT
PAPRIKA SALT
PESTO SALT
PEPPERCORN SALT
PORT SALT
RED WINE SALT
ROASTED GARLIC
    SALT
SAFFRON SALT
SEAWEED SALT
SESAME SALT

SHIITAKE SALT
SMOKED SALT
SRIRACHA SALT
SWEET SALT
SZECHUAN PEP-
    PERCORN SALT
TEA SALT
TRUFFLE SALT
VANILLA SALT
VINEGAR SALT
WASABI SALT

There are many things I love about salt. It's ancient. It's international. It's beautiful. It feels good. But the thing that I love most is also the most overlooked aspect of salt—it is a blank canvas onto which I can paint any flavors I choose. This creative aspect of infused salt is infinitely appealing to me. So is the fact that while I can buy infused salt in stores, I can make it better and cheaper at home.

The main ingredient in these recipes is, of course, salt. Sea salt is preferred (as opposed to mined salt, which I feel is too salty for most of these recipes), but the type and brand are up to you. Just be sure it is a natural, unrefined salt. (All the salts recommended in Part 2 are unrefined.) As you become more familiar with international salts, you will find one or two that you really like. Use those for your infused salt. If you plan to make a lot of infused salt (which I highly recommend) look for bulk bags of good sea salt at restaurant supply stores, or in Asian markets.

Once I have infused salt, I use it just as I would any finishing salt, adding a burst of flavor to the top of a dish, and a burst of complexity to the top of each bite. And it makes a great gift. Your hostess or secretary or teacher or secret Santa will be *way* more impressed with this than a boring bottle of wine.

agave salt

Agave syrup, like maple syrup, is made from a sugary sap. In this case it comes from the stalk of the maguey or century plant, a plant best known for its main product, tequila. The maguey's sweet sap runs when it comes into bloom; the stalks are gnawed for a sweet treat, like sugarcane. The flavor is reminiscent of tequila, and so, unsurprisingly, this salt goes everywhere tequila goes. Use it, first and foremost, on the rim of your margarita glasses. Then add it to ceviche, guacamole, salsa, carne asada, and fresh homemade tortilla chips. (Oh yeah, baby.)

INGREDIENTS

¼ cup agave syrup

1 cup unrefined sea salt

METHOD

1. Stir the salt and syrup together thoroughly. Spread it out in a thin layer on a dry baking sheet, set it in the sun, and dry for 1 to 2 days. Alternatively, you can place it in a dehydrator, or in an oven set at 100°F overnight, or until very dry.

VARIATIONS

—Agave Plus. Follow the Mexican theme with ½ cup of chopped fresh cilantro and the dried zest of 1 lime (see Citrus Salt, page 36). Or consider a teaspoon of ground cumin, coriander, or dried chiles. Or use them all for a salty flavor explosion to enhance your South-of-the-Border spread.

—Maple Syrup. Agave is not the only sweet syrup. Use the same technique with maple, or any other syrup you love and have. (Flavored Italian soda syrups come to mind.)

anchovy salt

Use this salt to finish crudités, pasta, Salad Niçoise, or your favorite pizza slice. See the variation under Caper Salt, page 34.

---

anise salt

The slightly sweet licorice flavor of anise seed (similar to but botanically different from, fennel), adds an exotic flair to a number of foods. Try it on seafood (shrimp, lobster, salmon), in Mediterranean dishes (tagines [see Glossary page 204], couscous, lamb), and in desserts (chocolate, caramel, autumn fruits). The method is the same as with any other dried spice salt, but this is such a wonderful salt that it deserves its own heading.

INGREDIENTS

¼ cup anise seeds

1 cup unrefined sea salt

METHOD

1. Toast the anise seeds in a hot dry skillet until popping and fragrant, about 30 seconds. Immediately pour them out of the pan and let them cool. Pulverize the seeds with ¼ cup of the salt in a coffee mill, pulsing to a uniform texture. Mix together with the remaining ¾ cup salt.

VARIATION

—Flavor Cousins. A similar flavor profile can be made by using toasted fennel seeds, or fennel pollen. You can even use fresh fennel fronds, which are typically discarded, but have huge flavor. In the case of fresh fennel fronds, follow the instructions for Fresh Herb Salt (page 40). You might also enjoy salt made from anise-flavored liqueurs, like Sambuca, Pernod, Ouzo, Arack, and the like. For these salts, follow the procedure for Bourbon Salt (page 33).

ash salt

Smoked salt is popular, as is anything with a smoky flavor. But the use of ash is popping up more and more, too. Mixed with a great coarse salt, ash makes a fantastic finish, and adds a hint of outdoor cooking (especially nice when you're stuck in a tiny apartment in winter). The world's top restaurants are harnessing the bitter smokiness of ash on everything from marinades and rubs to crunchy, crumbled garnishes for vegetables, soups, and desserts. The ash in question is typically made from an indigenous edible grass, herb, or wood. First-time ashers should use familiar edibles—rosemary, thyme, sage—dried in whole bunches, which you can do in your kitchen by hanging them upside down for a few days.

INGREDIENTS

1 large bunch dried rosemary, thyme, or sage

1 cup unrefined sea salt

METHOD

1. Place the dried plant material on a large sheet of aluminum foil. Working away from anything flammable, preferably in a barbecue or fireplace, light the material on fire. Hold a screen, frying pan, or lid a foot above the flame to catch any ash that may float away. Let it burn completely, then cool and transfer the ash to a small bowl. Add half the salt, mix to combine, then add the remaining salt. Store the salt in a jar with a tight-fitting lid for at least 1 hour before using, to concentrate the smokiness.

bacon salt

The epitome of salty, this smoky, meaty essence is great on top of potatoes, yams, spinach salad, and anything "maple-y," "chocolate-y," or "caramel-y." See the variation under Caper Salt, page 34.

bourbon salt

This is not a cocktail salt. Any bourbon drink that has salt around the rim will inevitably make you regret drinking it. This salt is, however, perfect for your best barbecued beef or pork, roasted sweet potatoes, or baked beans. And don't forget it on the sweet side. It's delightfully decadent in deep dark caramel, in pecan praline ice cream, on top of chocolate truffles, or dusted over a warm à la mode slice of apple pie.

INGREDIENTS

1½ cups bourbon, reduced by half and cooled

1 cup unrefined sea salt

¾ cup granulated sugar

METHOD

1. Have an oven mitt and a wet towel at the ready. Pour the bourbon into a small saucepan that has a tight-fitting lid. Set the lid nearby. Place the pan over medium heat and bring the bourbon to a simmer. Let it bubble as much as it can without boiling over, and cook in this manner until it has reduced by half (¾ cup). Be careful not to let it ignite. This amount of alcohol will take a long time to burn off, which can be a fire hazard. Smother a flame as soon as it happens, then try again. The key here is to keep the heat low enough to prevent a fire, but high enough to keep the bubbles popping on the surface, which is what causes reduction. When the liquid has reduced to ¾ cup, about 5 minutes, let it cool completely.

2. Combine the bourbon reduction, salt, and sugar in a food processor and pulse until the consistency resembles wet sand. (Depending on the success of your reduction, you might need to add a bit more salt at this point to achieve the wet sand consistency.) Spread out the mixture in a thin layer on a dry baking sheet, and set in the sun to dry for 1 to 2 days. Alternatively, you can set it in a dehydrator, or in an oven set at 100°F overnight, or until dry. When completely dry, break up any clumps with your fingers or a spoon, and transfer to a container with a tight-fitting lid.

VARIATIONS

—Boozy Options. Great results can be had using the same technique with Scotch, cognac, Armagnac, brandy, or dark rum. Other hard liquors, such as gin or vodka, have either too strong a flavor, or too unremarkable a flavor, to add much interest to a salt.

—Sweet Liqueurs. Grand Marnier, Sambuca, Cassis, Chambord, Limoncello, Kahlúa, and their ilk make terrific salts, which, when complete, are great finishing salts for seafood, fruit, and, of course, desserts. Use 1 cup of liqueur, reduced by half to ½ cup for every 1 cup of salt. Omit the sugar here, because these liqueurs are sweet enough.

caper salt

Like other cured foods, capers are already salty. But when mixed into a salt and used in a finishing capacity, they add an amazing burst that wakes up your palate, paving the way for the flavors that lie underneath. Capers are the buds of an evergreen shrub native to the Mediterranean. They come in a number of sizes, and are either pickled in a brine or dried and packed in salt. There are some cool jumbo varieties (caper berries), but I like to reserve those for garnish, because they look so great. Stick with the smaller capers for your salt.

INGREDIENTS

¼ cup capers, drained

1 cup unrefined sea salt

METHOD

1. Combine the capers and ¼ cup of the salt in a food processor or a mortar and pulverize to a paste. Transfer to a bowl and mix with the remaining ¾ cup salt until it resembles wet sand. Depending on the moisture of your capers, you may need to add more salt to achieve the wet-sand consistency. When all the salt is thoroughly covered, spread it out in a thin layer on a dry baking sheet, set it in the sun, and dry for 1 to 2 days. Alternatively, place it in a dehydrator, or in an oven set at 100°F overnight, or until dry. When completely dry, break up any clumps with your fingers or a spoon.

VARIATIONS

—Anchovy Salt. Use these salty fish for the same effect, replacing the capers with 2 anchovy fillets.

—Bacon Salt. Replace the capers with 1 strip of well-cooked bacon, that has been cooled and crumbled.

celery salt

This spice is a necessary ingredient in a classic Bloody Mary, the classic Chicago-style hot dog, retro version coleslaw, and it is one of the main ingredients in Old Bay Seasoning. It is classically made with celery seeds or lovage seeds. I have added dried celery leaves for a fresher twist. Use it in the classic ways, or try it on crudités, grilled chicken, poached salmon, or roasted root vegetables.

INGREDIENTS

1 cup fresh celery leaves

Zest of 1 lemon, removed with a peeler in strips

1 teaspoon celery seeds

1 cup unrefined sea salt

METHOD

1. Spread out the celery leaves and lemon zest in a thin layer on a dry baking sheet, set it in the sun, and dry for 1 to 2 days. Alternatively, you can place them in a dehydrator, or in an oven set at 100°F overnight, or until dry. (Read about Citrus Salt, page 36.) When the celery leaves and zest are brittle, combine them with the celery seeds and ¼ cup of the salt in a coffee mill and pulse to a uniform texture. Mix together with the remaining ¾ cup salt.

chipotle salt

If you want an ingredient to get popular, name a fast-food chain after it. Ten years ago the only people using chipotle chiles were chefs. Now they are everywhere, and in everything—and for good reason. These dried, smoked jalapeños add a rich complexity to the standard chile heat. Use this salt wherever you would like a little heat—grilled shrimp, cheesy grits, tropical fruit salad, chocolate truffles—you name it. See the variations for other chile salt options.

INGREDIENTS

3 dried chipotle chiles

1 cup unrefined sea salt

METHOD

1. Toast the dried chiles on a hot dry skillet, griddle, or in a hot oven until they are limp and fragrant, 3 to 5 minutes. (Be careful not to burn them.) Let them cool. As they do, they will crisp up. Remove the stem and the seeds. (You might want to wear gloves for this to keep the capsicum off your hands.) Grind the toasted chile flesh with ¼ cup of the salt in a coffee mill and pulse to a uniform texture. Mix together with the remaining ¾ cup salt.

VARIATIONS

—**Chipotle Options.** Sometimes I run across chipotle powder, but more often than not, the only chipotle I can find is in a can, slathered in adobo sauce. Luckily, we can make both of these options work. The powder is easy—just add it to salt and mix. For the canned chipotle, drain off the sauce, pulverize the chile, and add salt until the mixture looks like wet sand. Then spread out on a baking sheet and dry in the sun for 1 to 2 days, or until dry.

—**Chile Options.** You can use this method with any dried chile. New Mexico, pasilla, guajillo, ancho, whichever you love the most or have access to, can be made into an amazing salt. Just substitute your chiles for the chiles in the recipe above. If you need more heat than this recipe offers, feel free to increase the chile-voltage.

chocolate salt

Chocolate salt sounds weird, and it is. But weird is not necessarily bad. The bitter richness of the cacao bean enhances more than desserts. Try it on pot roast or brisket, roasted turkey, whole fatty fish, or baked beans. But don't rule out dessert. There is a sweet version in the variations that is perfect to finish all your chocolate, salted caramel, and vanilla recipes. Or try it sprinkled on fat, juicy, ripe dates. Yes, indeed.

INGREDIENTS

½ cup cacao nibs

1 cup unrefined sea salt

METHOD

1. Grind the nibs and with ¼ cup of the salt in a coffee mill and pulse to a uniform texture. Mix together with the remaining ¾ cup salt. Transfer to a container with a tight-fitting lid. Let it mature for at least an hour or two for the best flavor.

VARIATIONS

—**Sweet Salt.** Some chocolate salt recipes add sugar, which downplays the "cacao-ness," and accentuates the "chocolatey-ness." To do this, add 1 tablespoon of coarse, unrefined sugar to the coffee mill with the nibs.

—**Cocoa Powder Salt.** You can easily blend cocoa powder into a good salt for a similar effect. There are pros and cons to this. I find that it is too chalky for a finishing salt, although is works well in a spice-rub application. However, cocoa powder, unlike nibs, offers some variety in flavor. Ebony cocoa, which is used in Oreo cookies, makes an amazing salt for sprinkling across your cappuccino foam, or over really good vanilla ice cream. Add it to a good flake salt and let it mature for at least an hour or two for the best results.

—**Mexican Chocolate Salt.** Add to this recipe 1 inch of a good Mexican cinnamon stick and a small dried ancho chile. Grind these with the nibs.

—**Chocolate Vanilla Salt.** Add a scraped vanilla bean to this recipe with the second addition of salt and mix well. Spread it out in a thin layer on a dry baking sheet, set in the sun, and dry for 1 to 2 days. Alternatively, you can dry it in a dehydrator, or in an oven 100°F overnight, or until dry.

---

citrus salt

This is the most popular of the infused salts, probably because it is accessible (i.e., not weird) and can be used pretty much anywhere one would use straight salt. Meat, fish, vegetables, grains, fruits, and desserts are all brightened by the citrus punch. You can make it with any—and every—citrus fruit you can get your hands on. Then make it with a mixture. And if you want to be superfancy, try it with some of the more exotic citrus fruits, like the Buddha's hand or blood oranges. You really can't go wrong. See the variations for citrus salt combination ideas. A note about technique here: Some recipes call for the zest to be grated off the fruit using a microplane. I have found that such fine grating releases too much of the citrus oil into the air, rather than keeping it in the zest, which is where I want it. So invest a good, sharp potato peeler that doesn't take off too much pith, and remove the zest in larger strips. (This investment will probably set you back about $1.78.)

INGREDIENTS

2 large lemons, oranges, tangerines, limes, or 1 large ruby grapefruit

1 cup unrefined sea salt

METHOD

1. Using a sharp potato peeler, remove all the zest from your chosen citrus fruit in long strips. Spread the zest out in an even thin layer on a

baking sheet or tray and set it aside to dry for 1 to 2 days. If you can set it in a sunny place, the drying will happen faster. When it feels brittle, grind it with ¼ cup of the salt in a coffee mill and pulse to a uniform texture. Mix together with the remaining ¾ cup salt. Transfer to a container with a tight-fitting lid.

VARIATIONS

—**Tiny Fruits.** Kumquats and Key, or Mexican, limes make nice salt, too, but their zest is a little harder to access. I suggest using a very sharp paring knife to remove the zest in the biggest chunks possible. For the recipe above, you will need at least a dozen of these smaller fruits.

—**Citrus Herb and Spice Salt.** The following lists are merely suggestions, based on common usage. Feel free to use your own imagination, or mix and match. Use 1 to 2 tablespoons of chopped fresh herbs, and either dry them before adding with the dried zest, or mix them in wet and spread the entire batch of citrus-herb salt out in the sun to dry. For dry spices, start with 1 tablespoon, then add more if needed.

—**Lemon Combinations.** Pair your lemon with thyme, sage, parsley, mint, chervil, toasted cumin seeds, lavender, rosemary, chives, ginger, fennel fronds or toasted fennel seeds, toasted anise seeds, toasted sesame seeds, saffron, matcha, vanilla, or a mixture of peppercorns.

—**Orange Combinations.** Try rosemary, thyme, bay, sage, cayenne, cinnamon, allspice, cardamom, toasted coriander seeds, cacao nibs, fennel fronds or toasted fennel seeds, toasted anise seeds, vanilla, or espresso.

—**Lime Combinations.** Combine lime zest with cilantro, chipotle or other chiles, parsley, toasted coconut, toasted coriander seeds, toasted cumin seeds, toasted sesame seeds, matcha, or wakame. I particularly like coriander, chipotle, and lime.

—**Grapefruit.** Try rosemary, toasted coriander seeds, toasted sesame seeds, thyme, cilantro, lavender, or pink peppercorns.

curry salt

I love the exotic aroma of Indian food. Just now, typing this, my mouth started to water because I'm thinking about it. You could use this curry salt to finish off your own homemade curries, but in India they have a special salt for that already (see Kala Namak, page 19). I prefer to use this on foods in which the curry flavors are unexpected—egg salad, mashed potatoes, pretzels, grilled vegetables, sugar cookies, ambrosia salad. But it's your salt, so put it wherever you want.

INGREDIENTS

3 bay leaves

1 teaspoon cumin seeds, toasted and cooled

1 cup unrefined sea salt

1 tablespoon garam masala, chaat masala, or your favorite curry powder

METHOD

1. Combine the bay leaves and cumin seeds with ¼ cup of the salt in a coffee mill and pulse to a uniform texture. Mix in the curry powder and the remaining ¾ cup salt. Transfer to a container with a tight-fitting lid. Let it mature for at least an hour or two for the best flavors.

VARIATIONS

—**Mukhwas.** This is a sweet, fragrant mix of various seeds, herbs, and essential oils, served after an Indian meal as a breath freshener and digestive aid. You can usually find it in a small dish at the hostess station of your favorite Indian restaurant. It is made in a number of ways, and can include fennel seeds, anise seeds, sesame seeds, coriander seeds, betel nut, dried dates, and small colorful candies. As a salt, it gives an amazing burst of flavor. Use it to top mango sorbet, rose-scented custard, sweet rice pudding, or your best vanilla milk shake. You can find it online, or in markets that feature Indian ingredients. (See Artisan Salt Purveyors, page 207.) Use ¼ cup of mukhwas in place of the bay, cumin, and curry in this recipe.

dashi salt

This umami-rich broth base, made by simmering kelp (kombu) and dried fermented fish (katsuobushi) is the base of dishes such as miso soup and noodle broths. It is, in fact, the food that Kikunae Ikeda used to identify the fifth flavor, umami, in the early twentieth century. Dashi (see Glossary page 200) is already salty, but having it in a salt form adds a welcome layer of texture over fatty meat or seafood, fried eggs, roasted potatoes, grilled eggplant, wilted spinach, warm grains, and fresh shellfish.

INGREDIENTS

1 to 2 tablespoons instant dashi

1 cup unrefined sea salt

METHOD

1. Combine the dashi with ¼ cup of the salt in a coffee mill and pulse to a uniform texture. Mix together with the remaining ¾ cup salt. Transfer to a container with a tight-fitting lid.

VARIATIONS

—**Citrus Dashi.** Add 1 teaspoon of instant dashi to the preparation for Citrus Salt (page 36).

—**Shiitake Dashi.** Add 1 teaspoon of instant dashi to the preparation for Shiitake Salt (page 49) for an über umami effect.

date salt

Sprinkle this over curries, tagines, milk chocolate, or sautéed bananas. See the Sweet Salt variation on page 53.

dried herb and spice salt

Dried herb or spice salt is perfect to make when you have an abundance of herbs, either homegrown, or store-bought. On top of being superflavorful, salt made with dried herbs has the advantage of being really fast to make. So you can get inspired on short notice, or throw together an amazingly quick hostess gift. It's also a great vehicle for herb blends. My favorite is herbes de Provence, but it works just as well with an Italian blend, curry powders, za'atar (see Glossary page 201), sumac—any dried herb or spice you love. Try these versatile salts on cooked or fresh vegetables (they're great on crudités), salads, grilled meat and fish, or roasted root vegetables.

INGREDIENTS

½ cup dried herbs or spices

1 cup unrefined sea salt

METHOD

1. Grind the dried herbs or spices with ¼ cup of the salt in a coffee mill and pulse to a uniform texture. Mix together with the remaining ¾ cup salt. Transfer to a container with a tight-fitting lid. Let it mature for at least an hour or two for the best flavor.

VARIATIONS

—**Cardamom Salt.** Cardamom is my favorite spice, and it makes a salt that works equally well on spicy curries and fruit cobblers. Grind 5 to 6 cardamom pods with the coarse salt, then strain out the husks.

—**Mustard Salt.** Grind brown or yellow mustard seeds with the coarse salt for this tangy, spicy salt.

espresso salt

Sometimes called Navy coffee, adding salt to your cuppa Joe is thought by some to improve a particularly crappy brew by balancing bitterness or acidity. Using the same logic, I will frequently add coffee to rich foods—pot roast, pork belly, short ribs, barbecue rubs and sauces—for the balancing effect that the bitter bean adds. Coffee salt can similarly play an important role in the balance of flavor. A slight salty bitterness at the top of a taste will filter down around your palate and calm everything down. Try it not only on rich meats, but also in rich sauces, rich desserts, or anything that you think might be a little too heavy.

INGREDIENTS

¼ cup dark roast coffee beans

1 cup unrefined sea salt

METHOD

1. Grind the coffee with ¼ cup of the salt in a coffee mill and pulse to a uniform texture. Sift through a fine-mesh sieve to remove any large bean chunks. Mix together with the remaining ¾ cup salt. Transfer to a container with a tight-fitting lid. Let it mature for at least an hour or two for the best flavor.

VARIATION

—**Turkish Coffee.** This is also called Arabic coffee and Persian coffee. Whatever you call it, it is an amazing flavor combo. To this recipe add 4 to 5 cardamom pods with the coffee beans. You can add them whole if you want, because the husks will be sifted out. Use this to finish anything chocolate, or use it as a rub for beef ribs or barbecued lamb.

flower salt

Cooking with flowers was more popular in the Middle Ages and Victorian era than it is now. I aim to change that. These salts are not only fragrant, they are beautiful. Use them on chocolates, tropical fruits, creamy soups, or grilled lamb.

INGREDIENTS

½ cup dried pesticide-free lavender, rosebuds, cherry blossom, violets, or citrus blossoms

1 cup unrefined sea salt

METHOD

1. Grind the dried flowers with ¼ cup of the salt in a coffee mill and pulse to a uniform texture. Mix together with the remaining ¾ cup salt. Transfer to a container with a tight-fitting lid. Let it mature for at least an hour or two for the best flavor.

VARIATIONS

—**Rose Saffron.** This is my favorite salt for mango. Add a hefty pinch of toasted saffron threads with the first addition of salt. (See Saffron Salt, page 48)

—**Flower Water.** To make a flower salt using liquid essence, mix a tablespoon in with 1 cup of salt, then dry it in the sun.

fresh herb salt

Fresh herb salt has a decidedly different effect than a dried herb salt. It is not necessarily stronger (certain herbs are more potent after they dry), but it is fresher. I think of it in the same terms as adding a dollop of pesto to a recipe—it just wakes everything up. I use fresh herb salt on just about everything—meats and fish, vegetables and grains, pastas, potatoes, and fresh green salads. It is the one I use more than anything else. I like a blend of thyme, rosemary, sage, oregano or marjoram, tarragon, scallions or chives. But most of the time I make it with whatever fresh herbs are starting to look a little wonky in my fridge.

INGREDIENTS

1 tablespoon chopped fresh chives or scallions

1 cup fresh herb leaves

1 cup unrefined sea salt

METHOD

1. Grind the chives, herbs, and ¼ cup of the salt in a coffee mill and pulse to a uniform texture. Mix together with the remaining ¾ cup salt. Spread out in a thin layer on a dry baking sheet, set it in the sun, and dry for 1 to 2 days. Alternatively, you can place it in a dehydrator, or in an oven set at 100°F overnight, or until dry. When completely dry, break up any clumps with your fingers or a spoon, and transfer to a container with a tight-fitting lid.

VARIATIONS

—**Garlic Herb.** You can add garlic to the mix, too. Grind 1 garlic clove and ¼ cup of the salt together first and make a fine paste. Then add the herbs, grind again, and finally the remaining salt. Be sure this salt is completely dehydrated before storing airtight in a container.

garlic salt

See Roasted Garlic Salt, page 48.

ginger salt

It is possible to use ground dried ginger for this recipe (follow instructions for Dried Herb and Spice Salt (page 39), but if possible, I prefer to use a knuckle of fresh ginger. In this case, use a traditional ceramic ginger grater if you have one, which breaks down all the ginger pulp without any of the ginger fiber. A microplane grater, which shreds the fiber and adds it to the grated mass, is the second choice here.

INGREDIENTS

1 cup peeled and grated fresh ginger

1 cup unrefined sea salt

METHOD

1. Spread the grated ginger out in a thin, even layer on a dry baking sheet. Set it in the sun to dry for 1 to 2 days. Alternatively, you can place it in a dehydrator, or in an oven set at 100°F overnight, or until dry. When the ginger feels brittle, grind it to a fine powder in a coffee mill or mortar with ¼ cup of the salt and pulse to a uniform texture. Mix together with the remaining ¾ cup salt. Transfer to a container with a tight-fitting lid.

VARIATIONS

—**Ginger Sesame.** Add 2 tablespoons of toasted sesame seeds (white or black) to the grinder with the ginger.

—**Ginger Citrus.** Add the dried zest of 2 lemons to the grinder with the ginger.

—**Ginger Mint.** Add ¼ cup of dried mint leaves to the grinder with the ginger.

grand marnier salt

This salt is fantastic sprinkled over anything chocolate. See Bourbon Salt variations on page 33.

ROSE SALT

CHOCOLATE SALT

VANILLA SALT

hojicha salt

Also called *bancha*, this is my favorite tea of all time. As a salt it is fantastic over roasted poultry and grilled fish. See Tea Salt on page 54.

---

horseradish salt

The radish family is a big one, and it has some strong members—including wasabi and horseradish. These roots grow easily, and if you can get it from a farmer's market, or fresh from your yard, do so. Often these roots, when sold in larger markets, have been hanging around the store for a while, are very dry and woody, and have lost their kick.

INGREDIENTS

One 4- to 5-inch piece fresh horseradish root, peeled and roughly chopped

1 teaspoon white wine vinegar

1 cup unrefined sea salt

METHOD

1. Combine the horseradish and vinegar in a food processor and pulse. You may need to stop and scrape down the sides. Be careful! Good, fresh horseradish has potent fumes. Add ¼ cup of the salt and continue pulsing the machine until the mixture resembles a fine paste. Transfer to a bowl, combine with the remaining ¾ cup sea salt, and mix thoroughly. Spread the mixture out in a thin layer on a dry baking sheet, set it in the sun, and dry for 1 to 2 days. Alternatively, you can place it in a dehydrator, or in an oven set at 100°F overnight, or until dry. When completely dry, break up any clumps with your fingers or a spoon, and transfer to a container with a tight-fitting lid.

kale salt

For a bright vegetable essence, toast 4 leaves of chopped kale in a 350°F oven until crisp. Cool completely, then use it in place of seaweed in the Seaweed Salt recipe on page 49. Then try it again and add the dried zest of 1 lemon. Bam! Fantastic on veggie chips and popcorn.

---

li hing mui salt

I first had this tangy pink powder in Hawaii, dusted over my shaved ice. It is Chinese in origin, but has found a home in the Aloha State. It is a mixture of dried salted plums, licorice, salt, and sugar. It is already salty, but mixed with a good flake salt it makes a fantastic finish for extremely sweet foods—white chocolate, tropical fruits, flan—as well as a refreshing zing on top of a fruity cocktail. In Hawaii, the Li Hing Mui Margarita is all the rage. I find rimming the glass is too much for me, but I do enjoy a few big crystals of this finishing salt sprinkled on top.

INGREDIENTS

2 tablespoons Li Hing Mui powder

½ cup unrefined sea salt—try Cyprus Pyramid

METHOD

1. Stir together the powder and the salt, being careful not to crush any of the salt flakes. Transfer it to a container with a tight-fitting lid, set aside, and let it mature for at least an hour before using.

VARIATIONS

—Mexican Sweet Chili Salt. There is a popular Mexican candy called Lucas which is very similar to Li Hing Mui, but with the added zing of hot chiles. This has, however, been rumored to contain lead, and although it appears from time to time in the US, it is not recommended. But you can make your own version, with 1 teaspoon of dried red chiles, 1 teaspoon of brown sugar, ¼ teaspoon of citric acid, and ¼ cup of sea salt. Pulverize them together, then mix in ¾ cup of sea salt.

—**Pickled Sakura Cherry Blossom Salt.** Tea made from dried pickled cherry blossoms is a common sight at celebrations in Japan. The flowers are also frequently seen in desserts. They are salty, with a slight tang from plum vinegar, and a lovely floral essence. Combine ½ cup of dried pickled cherry blossoms with and ¼ cup of sea salt. Pulverize together, then mix it into ¾ cup of a good flake or pyramid salt.

maple salt

Maple salt is the perfect finish to all your autumnal favorites. There are two methods to choose from for this salt—wet (see variation of Agave Salt, page 32); and dry (see variations of Sweet Salt, page 53).

matcha salt

Green tea has taken the country by storm. It was first given to me twenty years ago by a student from Japan. He demonstrated the tea ceremony for me, and I fell in love with the entire ritual. Back then I had to go to downtown LA's Little Tokyo to find finely powdered matcha. Now I can get it at my corner coffeehouse. Used as a salt, it makes an amazing finish on fish, rice, and anything made with white or dark chocolate.

INGREDIENTS

1 tablespoon matcha

½ cup unrefined sea salt

1. Gently mix the matcha powder with half of the sea salt to break up the lumps. Then add the remaining salt.

mustard salt

For a punch on top of your pretzels or sausages, make this variation of Dried Herb and Spice Salt, page 39.

nut salt

The flavor of toasted nuts is hard to beat. They can enhance any meal of the day, and, unless you have a nut allergy, they should. Oatmeal, salads, steamed vegetables, and dessert will all benefit from a salty, nutty punch. When choosing nuts, consider their oil content. Macadamia nuts and pine nuts are notoriously oily, and as such, they tend to turn into butter. The oil will also limit the shelf life of these salts, so plan accordingly. Normally nuts can be stored for long periods in the fridge or freezer to prevent rancidity. But salt doesn't like moisture. So work in smaller batches.

INGREDIENTS

½ cup nuts—try almond, hazelnut, pistachio, or pepitas (which are not technically a nut, but are often used as such)

1 cup unrefined sea salt

METHOD

1. Toast the nuts until golden brown and fragrant. Cool completely, then combine with ¼ cup of the salt in a coffee mill and pulse to a uniform texture. Mix together with the remaining ¾ cup salt. Transfer to a container with a tight-fitting lid. Let it mature for at least an hour or two for the best flavor.

VARIATIONS

—**Spiced Nut Salt.** This mixture makes a great finish to oatmeal, breakfast pastries, or chocolate ice cream. Add the dried zest of 1 orange, 1 teaspoon of coffee beans, 1 teaspoon of brown sugar, ½ teaspoon of cinnamon, and 1 tablespoon of poppy seeds with the nuts and the first addition of salt. You can add any of these ingredients on their own, too.

—**Hot Nuts.** Add 1 teaspoon of your favorite chile powder for a spicy mix that works wonders on popcorn.

olive salt

Like bacon salt, olive salt sounds a lot like salt-salt. But the rich briny flavors of juicy green or black olives add a bit of umami deliciousness. Use good-quality olives from anywhere in the world—emphasis on good quality. Save the canned black olives for your fingertips. And be sure to scan the variations, because there is a wicked martini salt.

INGREDIENTS

3 to 4 large olives, drained

1 cup unrefined sea salt

METHOD

1. Combine the olives and ¼ cup of the salt in a food processor or mortar and pulverize to a paste. Transfer to a bowl and mix with the remaining ¾ cup salt until it resembles wet sand. Depending on the moisture of your olives, you may need to add more salt to achieve the wet-sand consistency. When all the salt is thoroughly covered, spread it out in a thin layer on a dry baking sheet, set it in the sun, and dry for 1 to 2 days. Alternatively, you can place it in a

dehydrator, or in an oven set at 100°F overnight, or until dry. When completely dry, break up any clumps with your fingers or a spoon, and transfer it to a container with a tight-fitting lid.

VARIATIONS

—**Martini Salt.** Use green olives, and add 1 tablespoon of juniper berries when you grind.

—**Tapenade Salt.** This ready-made olive spread has a nice balance of additional aromatics, usually including herbs, garlic, and anchovy. Just stir ¼ cup into to your salt, and dry as directed in the main recipe.

onion salt

For a nice finish to breads, meats, and roots, follow the instructions in the variation of Roasted Garlic Salt, page 48.

paprika salt

This powder, a specialty of Hungary, is made from a variety of dried red chile peppers. Hungarian paprika comes in a number of grades that range in color, sweetness, and heat. The Spanish make a great smoked paprika that is used in traditional paella. The generic stuff you find in most markets is incredibly boring when compared to these international varieties, and is only useful for adding color to your deviled eggs. If you have the opportunity, choose something that will add flavor, too.

INGREDIENTS

¼ cup best hot, sweet, or smoked paprika

1 cup unrefined sea salt

1. Gently mix the paprika with half of the sea salt to break up the lumps. Then add the remaining salt. Transfer to a container with a tight-fitting lid and set aside to mature for at least an hour before serving.

VARIATION

—**Paprika Chile Salt.** Increase the heat with the addition of 1 good dried chile pod. Use a dried ancho, guajillo, or chipotle chile, and grind it with ¼ cup of the salt before mixing it with the paprika and remaining salt.

pesto salt

Pesto is my back-up flavor. When I'm out of ingredients and I don't have shopping energy, I can always make something with the tub of pesto I keep on hand at all times. Once I figured out that I could do the same thing with salt, I began adding that essence to everything. Scrambled eggs, mashed potatoes, steamed vegetables, poached salmon, grilled steak—it's hard to go wrong. It is not technically pesto, because I like to avoid oil in infused salts when I can. The garlic and basil are the main attraction, and there are plenty of both.

INGREDIENTS

1 whole head garlic

¼ cup walnuts

1 large bunch fresh basil (2 to 3 cups leaves)

1 cup unrefined sea salt

METHOD

1. Preheat the oven to 400°F. Wrap the garlic head in aluminum foil and roast until tender, 30 to 45 minutes. Cool completely, then cut in half horizontally and squeeze out the softened garlic pulp. In the same oven, toast the nuts on a dry sheet pan until golden and fragrant. Cool these completely as well.

2. Roughly chop the basil, and place it in a food processor, blender, or mortar with the nuts and roasted garlic pulp. Process to a fine paste, then transfer to a bowl and stir in the salt. When all the salt is thoroughly covered, spread it out in a thin layer on a dry baking sheet, set it in the sun, and dry for 1 to 2 days. Alternatively, you can place it in a dehydrator, or in an oven set at 100°F overnight, or until dry. When completely dry, break up any clumps with your fingers or a spoon, and transfer it to a container with a tight-fitting lid.

peppercorn salt (a.k.a. salt 'n' pepa)

Let's talk about pepper, baby . . .

The world's most popular spice is, I fear, underappreciated. It is mostly sold and used already ground, but the effect of a freshly ground peppercorn is infinitely more interesting. Most peppercorn varieties come from the same plant—a climbing vine that is native to Indonesia and India. (It is not the same grape-like clusters that grow on ornamental willow-like trees in California and Florida, which can cause an allergic reaction.) Black peppercorns are harvested early, and dried. White peppercorns ripen on the vine, and then are hulled and dried. Green peppercorns are picked early and preserved in brine. Pink peppercorns come from a different plant native to Madagascar, (still not from the ornamental tree), and are slightly sweeter (and slightly more expensive). Szechuan peppercorns are actually seeds from a plant in the citrus family. Their flavor is slightly lemony, and they are more tingly and numbing than spicy hot.

INGREDIENTS

½ cup peppercorns (black, white, pink, Szechuan, or a mix)

1 cup unrefined sea salt

METHOD

1. Grind the peppercorns with ¼ cup of the salt in a coffee mill and pulse to a uniform texture. Mix together with the remaining ¾ cup salt. Transfer to a container with a tight-fitting lid. Let it mature for at least an hour or two for the best flavor.

VARIATION

—**Green Peppercorn.** Because these peppercorns are brined, this salt must be dried. Follow the instructions for Caper Salt, page 34.

port salt

Sprinkle this salt over roasted fresh figs, game meats, or dark chocolate. Use the variation in the following recipe for Red Wine Salt.

red wine salt

Wine salt, either straight or infused with herbs and spices (see the variations) is fantastic on anything with a strong umami characteristic. Try it on beef, lamb, mushrooms, artichokes, or save it for after the meal, sprinkled on triple cream cheeses, dried figs, and dark chocolate. A word of warning—like red wine itself, this salt will stain. I suggest you change out of your favorite white T-shirt before making it.

INGREDIENTS

1 750-ml bottle red wine (use the one you like to drink)

1 to 1½ cups unrefined sea salt

METHOD

1. Pour the wine into a large saucepan and bring it to a boil. Reduce the heat so that it is bubbling, but not boiling over, and cook until it has reduced to a thick syrup. There should be no more than 1 to 2 tablespoons of liquid remaining when reduced. Cool the syrup completely.

2. Combine the salt and the cooled wine syrup in a bowl and stir to combine. Add more salt as necessary to achieve the consistency of wet sand. Spread it out into a thin layer on a dry baking sheet, set in the sun, and dry for 1 to 2 days. Alternatively, you can dry the salt in a dehydrator, or in an oven set at 100°F overnight, or until dry. Transfer to a container with a tight-fitting lid.

VARIATIONS

—**Herbed Wine.** A sprig of fresh thyme or rosemary added to the pot while the wine is reducing will infuse the syrup with a complex savory element. The same can be done successfully with peppercorns or juniper berries. Strain the spice out before adding to the salt.

—**Mulled Wine.** Add cinnamon, peppercorns, star anise, and allspice to the reduction to give a wintery edge to this salt. Strain the spices out before adding the wine to the salt.

—**Port or Sherry.** Use the same basic method to make salt with these fortified wines.

roasted garlic salt

Roasted garlic is a sweet and creamy variation of the stinking rose, and improves the flavor of so many things, from meats to root vegetables to bread. It takes a while to cook, but it is well worth the effort. Added to salt, sweet fragrant roasted garlic is ready to be added to any dish, even as an afterthought.

INGREDIENTS

1 whole head garlic

1 cup unrefined sea salt

METHOD

1. Preheat the oven to 400°F. Wrap the head of garlic in aluminum foil and roast for 30 to 45 minutes until tender. Cool completely.

2. Cut the cooled head of garlic in half horizontally and squeeze out the soft pulp, which should now be a soft paste. Combine the garlic pulp and ¼ cup of the salt in a food processor and pulse to create a smooth puree. Transfer the puree to a bowl and mix with the remaining ¾ cup salt until it resembles wet sand. Add more salt if necessary to achieve a wet-sand consistency. When all the salt is thoroughly coated, spread it out in a thin layer on a dry baking sheet, set it in the sun, and dry for 1 to 2 days. Alternatively, you can place it in a dehydrator, or in an oven set at 100°F overnight, or until dry. When completely dry, break up any clumps with your fingers or a spoon, and transfer it to a container with a tight-fitting lid.

VARIATION

—Onions or Shallots. The same method can be used for oven-roasted onions or shallots. Wrap 1 medium onion or 2 to 3 shallots in aluminum foil and roast as directed, then process the same way.

saffron salt

These rust-red stigmas of the crocus are the most expensive spice in the world. They are difficult to harvest, with each low-growing flower producing only three threads. The bright golden color and grassy-floral fragrance that these threads emit have been used in textile dyes, in perfumery, and in the cuisines of many Eastern, Middle Eastern, and European cuisines. In a salt, saffron will enhance just about everything. Try it over grain dishes, stewed and grilled beef, lamb, sausages, shellfish, sweet custards, sorbets, and ice creams. When I make this salt I like to use a large flake or pyramid salt for maximum impact.

INGREDIENTS

1 generous pinch saffron threads

1 cup unrefined sea salt

METHOD

1. Toast the saffron threads briefly in a very hot, dry sauté pan until they are barely crisp, 10 to 20 seconds. Cool completely, then combine with ¼ cup of the salt in a coffee mill and pulse to a uniform texture. Mix together with the remaining ¾ cup salt. Transfer to a container with a tight-fitting lid. Let it mature for at least an hour or two for the best flavor.

VARIATIONS

—Saffron Lemon. Add the dried zest of 1 lemon to the saffron.

—**Saffron Fennel.** Add ½ teaspoon of toasted fennel or anise seeds to the saffron.

seaweed salt

Seaweed has long been a staple ingredient throughout the Far East. But in recent years it has made its way into American suburbia, not only wrapped around sushi, but in convenient snack packs, perfect for your lunch box. For this salt, use a seaweed that is easy to pulverize. (I find kombu to be too thick for this purpose.) Use the seaweed salt on anything that would benefit from its salty umami zing. I especially like it on fried potatoes and popcorn.

INGREDIENTS

1 sheet nori, or ¼ cup wakame, dulse, or arame

1 cup unrefined sea salt

METHOD

1. Combine the seaweed and ¼ cup of the salt in a coffee mill and pulse to a uniform texture. Mix together with the remaining ¾ cup salt. Transfer to a container with a tight-fitting lid. Let it mature for at least an hour or two for the best flavor.

VARIATION

—**Sesame Seaweed Salt.** Add 2 tablespoons of toasted sesame seeds to the grinder along with the coarse salt and seaweed.

sesame salt

These ubiquitous seeds (also known as benne seeds) come from the pod of a flowering plant native to Africa and India. The most commonly available are the white-tannish seeds, but they also are available in a number of colors, including black, red, gray, and brown. Try sesame salt on top of anything you would add sesame seeds to—stir-fries, dinner rolls, fried chicken, and even butterscotch pudding or chocolate ice cream. I like to use a mix of colors when I can.

INGREDIENTS

¼ cup sesame seeds

1 cup unrefined sea salt

METHOD

1. Toast the seeds briefly in a very hot, dry sauté pan until they are golden and fragrant, 20 to 30 seconds. Cool completely, then combine with ¼ cup of the salt in a coffee mill and pulse to a uniform texture. Mix together with the remaining ¾ cup salt. Transfer to a container with a tight-fitting lid. Let it mature for at least an hour or two for the best flavor.

VARIATIONS

—**Sesame Ginger.** You can add seeds to the Ginger Salt on page 41, or add 1 teaspoon of ground dried ginger to this recipe with the last addition of salt.

—**Sesame Wakame.** Grind 1 teaspoon of wakame seaweed with the seeds.

shiitake salt

There is nothing more savory than mushroom salt. And there is nothing more "mushroom-y" than shiitake mushrooms. Together, this flavor pair ramps up the umami of everything it touches. Perfect on already umami-rich meat, it also makes an interesting addition to less drool-inducing foods. Try it on red meat, then experiment with seafood, pasta, eggs, roots, custards, cream soups, and tofu.

INGREDIENTS

1 cup loosely packed dried shiitake mushrooms

1 cup unrefined sea salt

METHOD

1. Combine the mushrooms and ¼ cup of the salt in a coffee mill and pulse to a uniform texture. Mix together with the remaining ¾ cup salt. Transfer to a container with a tight-fitting lid. Let it mature for at least an hour or two for the best flavor.

VARIATION

—Mushroom Variety. There are many more types of dried mushrooms available, especially if you can find your way to an Asian market. Try porcini, morels, chanterelles, and anything else you can find dried. And, if you have a dehydrator, you can dry fresh mushrooms yourself.

smoked salt

Smoked salt is one of my favorite salts to cook with. It adds smokiness without the artificial aftertaste I find in liquid smoke. If you have a smoker, and frequently use it, this recipe is a no-brainer. Just place a tray of salt in with whatever else you are smoking. But if you have never smoked before, I think you'll find the process easy and addicting. Use the finished product on everything you might otherwise smoke—meats, fish, vegetables—then try it in more unusual ways. I like it on white chocolate, stone fruits, popcorn, and nut mixes (page 88). It's also great added into recipes like seafood chowder, vegetable puree soups, mac 'n' cheese, or your best salsa. By the way—if I'm firing up the smoker, I rarely do it for just one recipe. I will typically smoke meat, veggies, salt, and a tray of nuts. Why waste all that delicious smoke?

INGREDIENTS

2 to 3 cups wood chips, soaked in water for several hours, or overnight

2 cups unrefined sea salt

METHOD

1. Preheat your outdoor gas grill to 250°F. Place the soaked wood chips in a heatproof aluminum pan or smoke tray. Turn off all but one row of flame, and set the wood chips directly over the fire. Spread the salt out on a heatproof tray in a thin layer, and place in on the opposite side of the grill, away from the heat source. Close the lid and smoke for 1 to 2 hours at 200 to 250°F, until the salt turns dark gray. Cool completely, then break up any clumps by hand. I like to grind half of my smoked salt into a fine powder for use in recipes, and save the other half in coarse grains for finishing.

VARIATIONS

—Garlic Smoked Salt. Make the Roasted Garlic Salt (page 48), but instead of drying it in the sun, dry it in the smoker. Crazy good.

—Charcoal Grill. To smoke on this type of grill, it must have a tight-fitting lid. Build your fire on one side of the grill, and monitor the temperature periodically with an oven thermometer. Decrease the heat by keeping the lid ajar for a few minutes.

—Wok Smoke. Line a wok with a piece of aluminum foil large enough to extend above the rim by 3 to 4 inches. Place the soaked chips at the bottom of the wok, and fashion a small disk of foil that sits just on top of the chips. Add a wire rack and place the pan of salt (or whatever you want to smoke) on top. Cover with a generous amount of foil, leaving enough space above the salt for circulating smoke. Crimp the top foil tightly to the bottom foil to keep all the smoke inside. Place on high heat until smoke appears, then turn down to low and cook for about 30 minutes. Cool completely, then unwrap.

SMOKED SALTS

INFUSED HOT SALTS

sriracha salt

I can't explain the sudden popularity of this chile sauce. It's been around since the early twentieth century in Thailand, and has been available in the United States since 1980. The most popular brand in the U.S. is made by Huy Fong Foods, a company that was started by Vietnamese refugee David Tran. He named his company after the ship that brought him out of Vietnam. Also called "rooster sauce" because of the label design, demand has exceeded supply so much that Tran doesn't need to advertise. If you have jumped on the Sriracha bandwagon, this is the salt for you. Use it on anything that could use a spicy punch—popcorn, fried potatoes, ramen noodles, grilled seafood, and sliced tropical fruits. I like to use a big flaked salt for this one, but it works with any salt you choose.

INGREDIENTS

1 to 2 tablespoons sriracha sauce

1 cup unrefined sea salt

METHOD

1. Stir the chile sauce and the salt together thoroughly. Spread it out into a thin layer on a dry baking sheet and set in the sun for 1 to 2 days, until dry. Alternatively, you can dry it in a dehydrator, or in an oven set at 100°F overnight, or until dry. When completely dry, break up any clumps with your fingers or a spoon, and transfer it to a container with a tight-fitting lid.

VARIATIONS

—**Hot Sauce Salt.** You can use any chile or hot sauce you like for this recipe. My favorite is Green Tabasco!

—**Chile-Lime Salt.** Make a lime salt first (see page 36) then mix it with the chile sauce and dry as directed here.

sweet salt

The vibrant mouthfeel of sugar and salt is nothing new—as stated many times within this tome, sugar and salt are natural friends. Brown sugar bacon, prosciutto melon, salted candied pecans—these things are good for a reason. And so, if that's true, then why not add sweet-salt to everything? It's a valid premise. And while it might not fix everything, it is really great on popcorn, nuts, grilled meat, and those toastier flavors that seem to long for an extra zing. This recipe uses a pretty pedestrian brown sugar, but please see the variations for some *saaaweeeet* options.

INGREDIENTS

¼ cup unrefined brown sugar (turbinado, Sugar in the Raw, or chopped *piloncillo*)

1 cup unrefined sea salt

METHOD

1. Combine the sugar with ¼ cup of the salt in a coffee mill and pulse to a uniform texture. Mix together with the remaining ¾ cup salt. Transfer to a container with a tight-fitting lid. Let it mature for at least an hour or two for the best flavor.

VARIATIONS

—**Palm Sugar.** This sweetener is made from the sap of the palmyra date, or sugar palm, which is boiled down and sold either as a syrup, or in hard crystallized cakes. Use the cake form for making sweet salt. Chop it up into small hunks, then grind as directed above.

—**Date Sugar.** Date sugar has a hint of acidity, and an exotic flavor that works wonders on barbecued meats, highly spiced foods like curry, and tropical fruits. Unlike palm sugar, which is made from sap, date sugar is made from sweet dates that have been dehydrated and pulverized. And unlike the other sugars (and salt for that matter) date sugar does not dissolve. I enjoy the sweet texture as a finishing salt, but within recipes its texture may not be to your liking. Use it to replace the sugar in the main recipe.

—**Maple Sugar.** This sweet salt makes an amazing finish for all your autumnal cooking—pecan, apple, and sweet potato pies, roasted yams, candied nuts, popcorn balls, pumpkin soup, and especially anything caramel. Swap it out for the sugar in the main recipe.

—**Sweet Smoked Salt.** Use a smoked salt with any of these sugars for a woodsy sweet-savory finish.

—**Sweet Spiced Salt.** Add a mixture of cinnamon, nutmeg, cloves, allspice, ground ginger, cardamom, and star anise to the grinder with the sugar.

szechuan peppercorn salt

See Peppercorn Salt on page 46. Then try it with the addition of star anise and ginger (grind it with 2 pieces of star anise and 1 teaspoon of ground dried ginger), or use it as the salt in the Roasted Garlic Salt on page 48.

tea salt

There are literally hundreds of teas that would make an amazing salt. I like the classics best—hojicha, Darjeeling, and lapsang souchong—sprinkled on top of roasted duck, grilled fish, hearty grains, roasted root vegetables, vanilla *pot de crème*, and especially pistachio ice cream. But you should try it with all the teas you like. Hibiscus, chamomile, gunpowder, Earl Grey, chai, jasmine, Sleepytime—whatever floats your boat.

INGREDIENTS

¼ cup dried tea

1 cup unrefined sea salt

METHOD

1. Grind the tea with ¼ cup of the salt in a coffee mill and pulse to a uniform texture. Mix together with the remaining ¾ cup salt. Transfer to a container with a tight-fitting lid. Let it mature for at least an hour or two for the best flavor.

truffle salt

There are, in my opinion, few ingredients in the annals of culinary history as overhyped as the truffle. They are super umami, and mouth-wateringly good. But I am convinced that they are used, more often than not, because they are expensive. It's the culinary equivalent of "The Emperor's New Clothes." In most cases, I prefer a good shiitake for that fungal goodness. But if you find yourself with a truffle, you should get the most out of it, and this is a great way to extend that fungus's flavor life.

INGREDIENTS

1 tablespoon fresh black or white truffle, finely grated with a microplane

1 cup unrefined sea salt

METHOD

1. Combine the grated truffle and ¼ cup of the salt in a coffee mill and pulse to a uniform texture. Mix together with the remaining ¾ cup salt. Transfer to a container with a tight-fitting lid. Let it mature for at least an hour or two for the best flavor.

vanilla salt

If you think this is a salt meant for dessert, you'd only be half right. Sure, it's great on everything from the bakery and pastry kitchen. But it is also amazing on seafood, especially the sweeter shellfish.

INGREDIENTS

2 vanilla beans

1 cup unrefined flake sea salt

METHOD

1. Slice the vanilla beans in half lengthwise and scrape out the seeds with the tip of a sharp paring knife. (Combine the pods in a jar with dark rum and steep indefinitely for homemade vanilla extract.) Combine the vanilla seeds with the salt and mix thoroughly. Spread the mixture out in a thin layer on a dry baking sheet, set it in the sun, and dry for 1 to 2 days. Alternatively, you place it in a dehydrator, or in an oven set at 100°F overnight, or until dry. When completely dry, break up any clumps with your fingers or a spoon, and transfer to a container with a tight-fitting lid.

VARIATIONS

—Cinnamon Vanilla Salt. Before combining the vanilla seeds and salt, mix the salt with ½ teaspoon good-quality cinnamon. In addition to sweets, use this salt to finish curries, tagines, or anything mildly exotic.

—Rose Vanilla Salt. Before combining the vanilla seeds and salt, mix the salt with 2 tablespoons of dried rosebuds.

—Chocolate Vanilla Salt. Use the Chocolate Salt (page 36) as the salt in this recipe.

vinegar salt

For a tangy salt to finish fatty meats and fish, salads, and sweet fruits, use balsamic, red wine, champagne or a great fruit vinegar, and follow the method for Red Wine Salt on page 47.

wasabi salt

This hottest member of the radish family makes an amazing salt for vegetables, seafood, popcorn, and tropical fruits. It comes in several forms, including powder, paste, and as a fresh root. The powder is the easiest form to use here, but if you find yourself with a fresh root, follow the instructions for Ginger Salt, page 41.

INGREDIENTS

1 tablespoon wasabi powder

1 cup unrefined sea salt

METHOD

1. Gently mix the wasabi powder with half of the sea salt to break up the lumps. Then add the remaining salt.

VARIATION

—Szechuan Peppercorn Wasabi. For a crazy amazing tingly hot tongue sensation, grind 1 tablespoon of Szechuan peppercorns with half the salt, then continue with the recipe as written.

CURING
WITH SALT

P reservation is arguably the most important cooking technique ever devised. And in terms of great human accomplishments, it is, in my book, second only to agriculture. Preservation of food, especially meat, allowed for both political and economic expansion. The development of food preservation, like the domestication of plants and animals, meant that humans didn't have to gather fresh food every day. This, in turn, provided more time to pursue art, philosophy, science, and everything in between. It also allowed for longer journeys, which led to new discoveries, wars, and empires.

Today, because the food industry does the work for us, much of the art of food preservation has been forgotten. But all good things come back around, and there are a handful of food preservation societies popping up across the country. Here is my contribution to sustaining these classic methods.

While sun and smoke are likely the oldest techniques for preserving food, we are, of course, focusing here on the role that salt plays. Salt will dry food by leaching out its natural moisture through osmosis. It will also prevent bacterial growth by creating an unwelcoming saline environment. These simple functions are the basis for myriad recipes, preserving produce and animal flesh until they are needed, or wanted because they are out of season or out of reach.

PASTRAMI

CORNED BEEF

CORNED BEEF

Makes 4 to 5 pounds of meat; or a boiled dinner serving 4 to 6

In case you're wondering, corned beef has nothing to do with corn. "Corn" is an old term for grain (a fact that routinely confounds amateur food historians). It is used here in reference to an antiquated expression "a corn of salt," which is the original form of today's "grain of salt." All this to explain why the following recipe is nothing but salted beef. The basis for curing here is a brine. Brisket is probably the most commonly brined meat, but there are many other great things you can do with a brine like this. In addition to preserving the meat, a brine will tenderize otherwise dry cuts. And when spices and other aromatics are added, the flavor penetrates the meat, creating some rather tasty outcomes. See the variations for more briny ideas. I'm particularly fond of brining pork and turkey.

INGREDIENTS

1 gallon water

1 onion, roughly chopped

8 ounces unrefined salt—*I like coarse-grain rock salts for this, because they dissolve more slowly than sea salts. Try Himalayan or Bolivian. That said, I have made this successfully with sea salt, too.*

2 teaspoons Prague powder #1 (see Potassium Nitrate sidebar on page 60)

1 cup packed brown sugar

4 garlic cloves, minced

5 tablespoons Pickling Spice Blend (see recipe on page 60 for homemade)

One 4- to 5-pound beef brisket, trimmed of fat

2 large carrots, cut into large chunks

6 new potatoes

1 head green cabbage, trimmed and quartered

METHOD

1. In a large pot, combine half the water with the onion, salt, Prague powder, brown sugar, garlic, and pickling spices. Bring the mixture to a boil, then simmer until the salt and sugar dissolve. Remove from the heat and pour into a large container with at least a 1½-gallon capacity. Add the remaining half-gallon of cold water (or ice) and let it cool completely.

2. Add the meat, taking care to submerge it, which may require placing a plate on top to weigh it down. Refrigerate for 7 days, flipping the meat once a day to stir up the brine and ensure even absorption. The meat can live in the brine for a much longer time, but it takes about a week for it to become well brined. It should look tannish-gray on the outside, and pink on the inside (like raw meat).

3. Remove the meat from the brine, transfer it to another large container, and cover with cold water. Refrigerate for at least 8 hours, or overnight, to remove the excess salt.

4. Place the desalinated meat in a large pot, cover with cold water, place the lid on the pot, and simmer over medium heat for 30 minutes. Be careful not to let it boil, or the meat will toughen.

5. After 30 minutes, drain and refill the pot with fresh water. Repeat, bringing it just to a simmer. Add the carrots and potatoes and simmer for 30 minutes. Add the cabbage and continue to cook until everything is tender.

6. Transfer the meat to a cutting board and slice thinly, against the grain. Serve the sliced meat with the carrots, potatoes, cabbage, and a ladleful of the broth, which by now should have the perfect amount of saltiness. Accompany with Spicy Mustard (page 131) or horseradish. Use leftovers for corned beef hash, Reuben sandwiches (my favorite), or smoke it for pastrami (see the variations below)!

VARIATIONS

—**Turkey or Pork Brine.** Omit the Prague powder, and add 1 chopped onion and ¼ cup dried sage to the remaining brine recipe. (You may need to increase the recipe, depending on the size of your meat.) Submerge the bird or pork roast in the brine for 1 to 2 days, rinse well, and then roast as usual.

—**Pastrami.** Once your corned beef is brined and desalinated, give it a rub and a smoke. I like to mix a tablespoon each of black pepper, toasted and ground coriander, toasted and ground mustard seeds, paprika, garlic and onion powders, and brown sugar. Pat the meat dry with paper towels and rub the spices in well. Smoke the meat for 6 hours at 225°F or until it reaches an internal temperature of 160°F. Cool the meat completely, then chill it overnight. When you are ready to eat it, steam (or oven-braise) it very slowly for 2 to 3 hours, to an internal temperature of 205°F. (For smoking how-to, see the sidebar on page 000.) I have also successfully smoked a preboiled corned beef, but it turned out a bit tougher.

POTASSIUM NITRATE

Cured meat recipes often call for Curing Salt, Prague Powder, Instacure, or Saltpeter. They all contain Potassium Nitrate, which inhibits the growth of botulism bacteria, and preserves the meat's appealing red color. Used since ancient times, Saltpeter's unpredictable results are now regulated with the addition of sodium chloride (table salt) in Prague Powder and Instacure. Each brand carries a label of #1 or #2. Use #1 for short-term cure recipes (like those in this chapter). Use #2 for long-term dry-cures which breaks down more slowly. Use of those salts in other foods would be toxic, so they were colored pink to distinguish them from table salt. But the popularity of pink rock salt still makes it confusing. So the moral of the story is—label it well and keep it separated from your fancy salt.

PICKLING SPICE BLEND

Makes about ½ cup pickling spices

Homemade pickling spice is fun because it can be customized. Make it sweeter, spicier, herbier—it's entirely up to you. The following is my preferred mix, but feel free to adjust it to your taste.

INGREDIENTS

2 cinnamon sticks

2 star anise pods

1 tablespoon mustard seeds

5 bay leaves, crushed

2 tablespoons black peppercorns, crushed

2 tablespoons dill seeds

2 teaspoons juniper berries, crushed

1 teaspoon allspice berries, crushed

1 teaspoon ground dried ginger

1 teaspoon crushed cardamom pods

½ teaspoon crushed whole cloves

METHOD

1. Have a pot with a lid at the ready. Toast the cinnamon and anise by holding each of them over a flame with tongs until they ignite. Let them burn a minute, then drop them in a pot and cover to smother the flame. Cool, then crush in a coffee mill or mortar with a pestle.

2. Toast the mustard seeds in a hot, dry skillet for about a minute, until fragrant. Cool completely, then crush them in a coffee mill, or by hand in a mortar with a pestle.

3. Toss together the toasted ground spices with the remaining ingredients. Store in an airtight container at room temperature.

FARMER'S CHEESE

Makes 3 to 4 cups curd

While this is not technically curing, it is a form of preservation, so I have included it here. Fresh cheese is high on my list of most-favorite-things-ever to make. It can be so many things—spread on crackers, aged for a creamier texture, or used fresh as a filling for everything from crepes to raviolis to empanadas. Also, it's a great way to impress your friends. (I'm big on that.)

INGREDIENTS

1 gallon whole milk (cow or goat)

1 cup fresh lemon juice

1 teaspoon unrefined salt—*try any fleur de sel, sel gris, Sal de Maras, or a salt infused with wine, port, sherry, mushroom, citrus, ash, herbs, olives, capers, roasted garlic, peppercorns, or za'atar*

METHOD

1. In a large saucepan, heat the milk to 100°F. (Use a thermometer, or take it to just above body temperature—when it gets too hot to hold your finger in it.) Turn off the heat, stir in the lemon juice, and let it sit for 5 to 10 minutes until the curds separate from the whey. If your curds seem too small, you can add a little more lemon juice, as acid content in lemons varies.

2. Pour the mixture through a colander that has been lined with a double layer of wet cheese-cloth. It will take a while for all the whey to drain out, so be patient, and don't try to rush it by pushing or stirring. Let gravity do the work—it will yield better-size curds. Set the colander in a bowl, cover loosely with plastic wrap or a towel, then place in the fridge for at least 1 to 2 hours, to drain out all the whey.

3. Gather up the corners of the cheesecloth, tie it, and hang it in your fridge. (I just unfold a paper clip and hang it from the side of the top shelf.) Let it hang overnight, with a small plate underneath to catch any residual whey drips.

4. Unwrap the cheese and place in a bowl. Add the salt and toss until well incorporated. (See variations for more flavor options.) At this point you can enjoy this cheese's ricotta-like texture.

5. To age it, pack the cheese into molds. Line ramekins or plastic tubs with a single layer of wet cheesecloth. Fill the tub with your seasoned cheese and pack it in tightly. Wrap the ends of cheesecloth over the top. Refrigerate for 5 to 7 days. The longer it ages, the creamier the texture will be.

To serve, unmold the cheese on a plate and accompany with crackers or sliced baguette.

VARIATIONS

—**Flavors.** When adding the salt, add some additional flavors. Try fresh herbs, sautéed onions, toasted and ground spices (curry, za'atar, herbes de Provence), citrus zest, chopped olives, or a mushroom duxelles (see Glossary page 201).

—**Lining.** Instead of cheesecloth, the mold can be lined with grape or fig leaves (store-bought or freshly picked and blanched in boiling water. You can also coat the interior of the cheesecloth with dried herbs, spices, or ash.

BASTURMA

Makes 1 to 2 pounds cured beef

Also often referred to as *pastirma*, this terrific Armenian dry-cured beef is one of my favorite things to have on hand. It makes a terrific *mezze* snack just as it is, accompanied by cheese or pickled vegetables. But I especially love to throw it into recipes like scrambled eggs or cheesy noodles. It takes time to make, for sure. So much time that you'll forget you are making it—which makes the outcome that much more wonderful!

INGREDIENTS FOR STEP 1

1 to 2 pounds filet mignon or beef back loin

½ cup unrefined salt, finely ground—*I prefer rock salt for this, because the hard grains take their time dissolving. Try Persian blue or Himalayan.*

INGREDIENTS FOR STEP 2

20 garlic cloves (about 2 heads), peeled

1 red bell pepper

¼ cup fenugreek seeds

½ cup hot paprika

1 tablespoon ground allspice

An additional 2 teaspoons unrefined salt—*use the same salt criteria as above*

1 teaspoon freshly ground black pepper

1 teaspoon cumin seeds

½ teaspoon cayenne pepper

1 cup cold water

METHOD

1. Rinse the beef with cold water and pat dry with paper towels. Cut the loin into two equal pieces, then pierce it all over the surface with the tines of a fork. Coat the exterior with the salt, place it in a roasting pan, and weigh it down with a cast-iron pan or a very heavy plate. Let sit for 3 to 4 days in a cool spot (under 75°F), or in the fridge. Turn the meat once a day, draining off liquid as necessary.

2. After the 3 or 4 days, wash off the salt and soak the meat in cold water for 1 hour. Pat dry with paper towels. Wrap the meat in cheesecloth and hang in the fridge for 3 days. I usually rig a hook by hanging an open paper clip to the edge of an upper shelf of the fridge. It is important that air can flow freely around the meat, so don't cram it in. Some chefs like to thread through the middle of the meat with butcher's twine, then tie the ends in a loop to facilitate hanging later. I usually just hang it by the ends of the cheesecloth.

3. After 3 days of hanging, make the spice mix (known as chaiman, or chemen, blend): In a food processor, combine the garlic, bell pepper, fenugreek, paprika, allspice, salt, black pepper, cumin, and cayenne. Pulse to create a paste, adding water, a little at a time, as necessary to reach a spreadable consistency. Cover the entire surface of the meat with the paste, rubbing it in thoroughly. (You might want to wear latex gloves for this.) Rest the meat for another 2 weeks, again in a cool dry place, turning every day and making sure it is always covered in paste.

On the third week, wrap the meat again in cheesecloth and hang in the fridge for 1 more week, allowing the air to circulate freely. At this point, the meat should be very dense and dry. Slice thinly, like a piece of bacon, and serve as is, or use it in recipes.

BASTURMA

SWEET FENNEL PICKLES

SWEET CARROT PICKLES

SWEET RHUBARB
PICKLES

SWEET WATERMELON PICKLES

CLASSIC DILLY PICKLED
VEGETABLES

PICKLED BEETS

CLASSIC DILLY
PICKLED VEGETABLES

QUICKEST CUCUMBER PICKLES

BEET PICKLED EGGS

Makes 6 pickles

It is well known in my house that I am a beet lover. I like them in all colors, and in all applications. I even like their greens. (Correction—I *love* their greens.) So it will come as no surprise that I love these pickles. They are very sweety-beety, and they make a beautiful presentation. But if you're not a beet fan (like the rest of my family), you should skip this one. I have never been able to convince my brood that beets are where it's at. At some point, one just needs to move on. (Plus, more for me!)

INGREDIENTS

2 large beets, trimmed

6 hard-boiled eggs, peeled

2¼ cups rice vinegar or apple cider vinegar

¾ cup water

½ cup granulated sugar

1 garlic clove, minced

5 black peppercorns, roughly crushed

1 tablespoon unrefined salt—*try Bali Pyramid, Arabian fleur de sel, Manzanillo, or a salt infused with mustard, peppercorns, wasabi, or dried herbs*

METHOD

1. Preheat the oven to 375°F. Wrap the beets in aluminum foil and bake until they are tender, about 1 hour. Cool completely, then roughly chop them. Combine the beets in a sealable container with the hard-boiled eggs.

2. In a saucepan, combine the vinegar, water, sugar, garlic, pepper, and salt. Bring the mixture to a boil, then remove from the heat and pour it over eggs and beets. Let the liquid cool at room temperature, then refrigerate for at least 2 days. The longer the eggs cure, the pinker they will get. However, if they cure too long they will get rubbery. So limit the cure to 4 days max.

3. To serve, drain the eggs, pat dry, and cut into quarters or slices to highlight the gradation of color. Use on salads, as you would use hard-boiled eggs, or feature them on a canapé.

CLASSIC DILLY PICKLED VEGETABLES

Makes about 2 quarts pickles

I first saw these gems as a kid in the Italian delis of San Francisco's North Beach. Later, I was enamored of a similar concoction smothered over cold cuts in the New Orleans specialty, muffaletta. Once I figured out how easy they were to make, I have been unstoppable. There are many versions, some sweeter or tarter than others, but you can easily adjust the recipe below to suit your taste.

INGREDIENTS

6 cups assorted seasonal vegetables—including carrots, cauliflower, peppers (bell or otherwise), fennel, artichoke hearts—washed, trimmed, or peeled, and cut into 1-inch pieces

10 garlic cloves, halved

1 cup fresh dill (or fennel)

2 cups rice or apple cider vinegar

2 cups water

MEAT, PICKLES, AND CHEESE HORS D'OEUVRES

Makes about a dozen appetizers

Once you have a pantry full of cured foods, you will constantly be looking for ways to enjoy them. This is one of my favorite snacks. Sometimes I don't even bother with the skewers—can get them into my mouth faster that way.

INGREDIENTS

¼ pound (at least 12 pieces) thinly sliced cured meat—*try pastrami, basturma (page 62), prosciutto, or smoked ham*

8 ounces Farmer's Cheese (page 61) or goat cheese

12 to 14 pieces Sweet Rhubarb and Watermelon Pickles (page 67), cut into 1-inch lengths

4 large fresh Black Mission figs, cut into quarters—*or try other seasonal fruits, like plums, peaches, persimmons, or pears.*

METHOD

1. Working on a plate or cutting board, lay out a thin piece of cured meat. Spread a quarter-size dollop or slice of cheese in the center. Add a slice of rhubarb or watermelon pickle, then a fig quarter. Wrap the meat around to conceal all, then run a skewer through the center. Repeat with remaining ingredients, arrange on a platter, and chill until you are ready to serve. If you want, you can finish them with a pinch of a flake or pyramidal salt.

GRAVLAX

Makes enough cured salmon for 3 to 4 dozen servings

When I learned this recipe in culinary school, I thought I had unlocked the secret of the Universe. Curing fish in the kitchen of my tiny apartment made me feel very powerful, and—let's face it—a little cocky. It was ridiculous because, as you will see, the recipe is crazy simple. But until the "oohs" and "ahhs" stop (they never have), I'm doing my superior dance. Now you can, too.

INGREDIENTS

Two 1- to 2-pound salmon fillets, scaled and deboned, skin on

Grated zest and juice of 2 lemons

2 tablespoons olive oil

2 tablespoons brandy

1 cup packed brown sugar

½ cup unrefined salt—*try Læsø, Maldon, alaea, a smoked salt, or a salt infused with lemon, dill, anise, fennel, or peppercorns*

1 tablespoon black or white peppercorns, crushed

1 bunch fresh dill, chopped (about 1 cup)

METHOD

1. Wash the salmon, and pat it dry with paper towels. Mix together the lemon zest and juice, olive oil, and brandy and brush it on the pink meat of the fish. In a small bowl, mix together the sugar, salt, peppercorns, and dill. Spread this mixture on the pink meat of the fish.

2. Lay a large piece of plastic wrap, twice as long as your salmon, on your work surface. Place 1 piece of the coated salmon, skin side down, onto the plastic wrap. Then place the second piece on top, skin side up. What you have is a salmon sandwich, with the salt-cure in the center, and the skin on the outsides. Wrap the ends of the plastic wrap around the fish, sealing it tightly. (Use more plastic wrap if you need to.) Place your salmon package in a large pan (like a roasting pan) and weigh down the top with a plate and a couple of canned foods. Refrigerate for 3 days, turning the salmon every 12 hours. (This gives gravity a chance to help your cure.)

3. When the curing is complete, the flesh will be leathery, firm, and darker orange. Rinse off all of the cure with cold water, and pat the salmon dry with paper towels. Use a slicing knife (see Glossary page 202) to remove the salmon skin. Then cut the salmon with the grain, on a slight bias, and arrange in a fanned pattern on a platter. Serve with thinly sliced pumpernickel bread and a variety of condiments, including crème fraîche or sour cream, capers, chopped purple onion, or chopped fresh chives. Alternatively, use the leftover on a bagel the next morning, generously slathered with cream cheese, and layered with tomato and purple onion.

VARIATIONS

—Fennel Cured Gravlax. Replace the peppercorns with fennel seeds, the dill with chopped fennel (bulb and fronds), and the brandy with Pernod, Sambuca, or another anise-flavored liquor. Delish!

—Salt Block Gravlax. Salt block salmon is fun, but is not easier or better than the traditional method. Use just one piece of salmon, treated the same way, but omit the salt. Sandwich it between two salt blocks and wrap the entire assemblage in plastic wrap. Place it in a roasting pan, as before. Curing is usually faster, but look for the same leathery, firm, orange flesh before you rinse and serve. The weight of your block is the deciding factor.

CITRUS SALT CURED SEAFOOD

Makes about 4 servings

Gravlax is a very familiar salt-cure recipe, but the same method can be used successfully with other fish. Curing times vary, so look for signs of doneness—dense texture and darkened color.

INGREDIENTS

½ cup unrefined salt—*try a sel gris, Saltverk, a smoked salt, or a salt infused with citrus, seaweed, fennel, celery, saffron, wasabi, or chile*

1 cup granulated sugar

Grated zest of 3 lemons, limes, oranges, or a combination

1 pound fresh scallops, tilapia, trout, shrimp, or other firm, fatty fish, rinsed, dried, and sliced into a uniform ½-inch thickness

METHOD

1. In a small bowl, combine the salt, sugar, and zest. Place a large piece of plastic wrap on your work surface and spread half the salt mixture in the center. Lay the prepared fish on top, and cover with the remaining salt. Wrap the ends of the plastic wrap over the top and seal. (Use more plastic wrap as needed.) Place the wrapped fish in a baking dish and place a plate on top to weigh it down. Refrigerate for 12 hours, or overnight.

2. Check the fish the next day, and continue to cure, if necessary, until the color has darkened and the texture is firm. Check the fish every 4 to 6 hours. This may take as long as 3 days, depending on the fish.

3. Rinse the cured fish in cold water, and store, refrigerated, until you are ready to serve. Add it to salads, pastas, canapés, or slice thinly and serve as charcuterie.

SALT COD

Baccalà, bacalao, bakaliáros, bakkeljauw, saltfiskur, tørfisk, and *makayabu* are just a few of the world's names for salt-cured cod. A staple for centuries, salt cod was a hot commodity in the Middle Ages. It is relatively unused in the United States today, unless your family has recently immigrated from a cod-loving country. Even then, it is somewhat of a luxury item. (Sad that salt cod is expensive but a Big Mac is cheap . . . but that's another book.) This recipe is not the end of the line. Once you cure the cod, you are ready for a plethora of recipes, including combining it with mashed potatoes for *brandade* (see Glossary page 199), or frying it as croquettes. You can try it the Caribbean way, sautéed with *ackee* fruit (see Glossary page 199) and Scotch bonnet chiles, or sauté it with garlic and olive oil in the style of the Basque *Pil-Pil*. There is really no limit to great, classic salt cod dishes.

INGREDIENTS

1 pound cod fillet, skin removed, rinsed, and patted dry

2 to 3 cups unrefined sea salt—*try a sel gris, flor de sal, Mayan, or Piran*

METHOD

1. Line a deep baking dish with ½ inch of salt. Place the cod fillets on top, then cover the fillets with the remaining salt. Be sure they are completely covered. Cover loosely with plastic wrap and set in a cool place (50-65°F), or the refrigerator, for 2 days.

2. On the third day, rinse off all the salt from the fillets with cold water and pat the fish dry with paper towels. Wrap in a single layer of cheesecloth, set on a baking dish fitted with a rack, and return to the fridge for 7 to 10 days, or until the fish is dry and firm. At this point, it is ready to use, or store for later.

3. When you are ready to use your salt cod in recipes be sure to rinse it well and soak it in cold water for 24 hours, changing the water at least once. This will leach out the excess salt, and return it to a tender, flaky fishy texture.

SALT COD RECIPES

—Brandade. Simmer the desalinated fish slowly in milk, herbs, and a handful of garlic cloves until tender. Flake it and mix it with an equal amount of roughly mashed potatoes. Season with nutmeg, olive oil, and more salt if needed. Transfer to a baking dish and smooth the top. Layer the top with heavy cream, bread crumbs, and a few teaspoons of butter. Bake at 400°F until bubbly, about 20 minutes. Serve with sliced toasted baguette or crackers.

—Fish Cakes. The potato mixture above can be seasoned in any number of ways, then panfried as a fish cake, or rolled into a ball and deep-fried as a croquette. (In Central America, for instance, you often see cilantro added to the mix.) Use your imagination.

PIPIKAULA (HAWAIIAN JERKY)

Makes about ¾ pound jerky

Hawaii has a surprising cowboy culture. In the early 1800s, George Vancouver gave five longhorn cattle to King Kamehameha, who promptly set them free to roam the island. The herd multiplied into the thousands, and experts were called in to help control them—the Mexican vaqueros. They brought with them the horseman's skill and its related arts, including leatherwork, metal work, and guitar music (which evolved into ukulele music). By the mid-twentieth century half of the island lands were devoted to the cultivation of beef. Today that number has diminished, but the Hawaiian cowboy traditions linger on. This recipe is a favorite trail snack of these *paniolos* (see Glossary page 202).

INGREDIENTS

2 pounds flank steak

½ cup soy sauce

2 tablespoons alaea salt

2 tablespoons raw or brown sugar

1 garlic clove, minced

One 1-inch piece fresh ginger, peeled and grated

¼ to 1 teaspoon crushed red pepper flakes

1 tablespoon apple cider vinegar

¼ cup pineapple juice

METHOD

1. Slice the beef into thin strips (about ⅓ inch thick). Combine in a large bowl with the remaining ingredients, and toss to thoroughly coat. Marinate overnight in the refrigerator.

2. Drain the marinade off the meat. Spread the beef strips out in a single layer on a dehydrator tray, or on a baking sheet that has been lined with a drying rack. Dehydrate for 24 hours, or bake at 175°F for 5 to 8 hours, until very dry. Store airtight.

TUNA JERKY

Makes about ¾ pound jerky

This is fantastic cocktail food. And, of course, because it's jerky, it's good on the trail. (Especially if your trail is in Hawaii.)

INGREDIENTS

2 pounds tuna, snapper, trout, bass, or other firm-fleshed fish, cut into strips about ¼ inch thick

2 cups pineapple, finely chopped (you can also use canned crushed pineapple with the juice)

2 garlic cloves, chopped

1 tablespoon brown sugar

1 teaspoon freshly ground black pepper

¼ teaspoon cayenne pepper

2 garlic cloves, minced

One 1-inch piece fresh ginger, peeled and grated

1 teaspoon unrefined salt—*try a Hawaiian salt, a Japanese shio, a smoked salt, or a salt infused with roasted garlic, dashi, seaweed, sesame, Szechuan peppercorns, or chile*

METHOD

1. Toss all ingredients together, place in a zipper bag and refrigerate overnight (at least 12 hours).

2. Place a wire rack on a baking sheet, and coat it well with pan spray. Drain off the marinade and arrange the fish on the rack. Cook at 150°F for 2 hours, then turn the temperature down to 130° F (or open the oven door) and continue cooking, for another 2–4 hours, until dry, but not crisp. Cool completely, then store airtight in the refrigerator.

VARIATIONS

—**Dehydrator and Smoker.** This jerky dries better in a dehydrator, and has more flavor when made in a smoker. If you have either of those contraptions, by all means, go for it. Follow the manufacturer's instructions, and use the same guidelines for temperature and doneness.

—**Commercial Sauces.** The addition of store-bought teriyaki, barbecue, or chile sauce to your marinade will certainly work. Most contain a lot of sugar, so consider omitting the brown sugar from the recipe.

TUNA JERKY

PIPIKAULA

KIMCHI

Makes about 4 quarts kimchi

Though I have been to Korea, and have Korean friends, I was first taught to make Kimchi by a Belgian, Pascal Baudar. A Southern California foraging guru, Pascal's Kimchi is less about cabbage, and more about wild foraged greens. This is a more classic version, but see the variations for some interesting green alternatives. I use a kimchi pot made by another friend, Chef Glen Ochi—who is a potter and soap maker when he is not teaching culinary arts. But, if you don't have a kimchi pot you can still make your own kimchi. See the instructions in the variation for Jar Kimchi.

INGREDIENTS

2 tablespoons coarse unrefined salt—*use sogum, (Korean Kimchi Salt) or any coarse sea salt*

1 quart water

1 head garlic, cloves peeled and chopped roughly

4 scallions, chopped

1 to 3 teaspoons dried Korean chile (or red chili flakes)

One 1-inch piece fresh ginger, peeled and chopped

1 yellow onion

1 pound daikon (Korean radish or Mu), which is about half of a large daikon

1 head Napa cabbage

METHOD

1. Combine the salt and water, and set aside, stirring occasionally, until the salt has dissolved.

2. Using a mortar and pestle, or a food processor, puree the garlic, scallions, chile, and ginger into a rough paste. Transfer to a large bowl.

3. Thinly slice the yellow onion, daikon, and cabbage and add to the bowl. Add the saltwater (which should now be a brine) and begin kneading and squeezing the cabbage until it wilts. (You might want to wear latex gloves here.)

4. Transfer the vegetables to a kimchi pot, and press down so that the brine rises up to cover the vegetables. Place a weight on top (most kimchi pots come with a ceramic weight), so that there are no vegetables floating on the surface. Put the lid on and fill the rim with water. (Kimchi pot lids have a gutter for water, which keeps the bad stuff out while letting the internal gas from fermentation escape.) Leave the pot at room temperature for 3 days, replacing the water on top as necessary. On the third day, open the lid and taste your kimchi. If it tastes good to you, transfer it to airtight containers and store in the refrigerator. If it lacks excitement, leave it to cure for another day. (If it tastes horrible, well, something went wrong, or you just don't like kimchi.) Serve it alongside your Korean barbecue, put it on your hot dog (which you can now call a Kogi Dog as we do here in LA LA Land), add it to your noodles (hot or cold), fried rice, or scrambled eggs.

VARIATIONS

—Jar Kimchi. If you lack a kimchi pot, use large canning jars. Press the vegetables under the brine and weight it using a superclean, sterilized rock. (I run mine through the dishwasher.) Put the lid on and continue with the instructions as written.

—Veggie Additives. Try a variety of greens such as chard, beet greens, mustard greens, kale, wild curly dock, lambs quarters, watercress, or a mixture of cabbages. Vary the onions with shallots, leeks, and garlic chives. Or add grated carrot, sliced cucumbers, any kind of radish, fresh chiles, and sweet peppers. Just be sure you have at least 30 percent cabbage for the proper texture.

PRESERVED LEMONS

Makes about 1 quart preserved lemons

I feel that if I didn't include a recipe for preserved lemons, in a chapter about curing and in a book about salt, I would be remiss. That said, what could I possibly add to the hundred thousand interpretations of this recipe? Probably not much. There has already been plenty written on preserved lemons and their history in the cuisine of Northern Africa. I can tell you that I have a lemon tree in my backyard, and this recipe is an annual event. I first made them from a Paula Wolfert recipe in the late 1980s. The restaurant I worked at, Zola's, in San Francisco's Hayes Valley, was one level-head away from erecting a shrine to Ms. Wolfert. Now I am a Southern California resident, and we are all well versed in preserved lemons here. At a certain point you either need to preserve them or let them rot off the tree. I use this North African condiment (also found in some Indian regions) to add a salty tang to tagines, pilafs, stews, salads, and cocktails. I have even been known to serve them over vanilla ice cream. If you are new to preserved lemons, try adding them anywhere you might use a caper or anchovy.

INGREDIENTS

8 large lemons, washed and quartered

2 cups unrefined salt—*try flor de sal, Mali, Atlas Mountain, or a salt infused with citrus, sweet spices, herbs, peppercorns, or chiles*

1 tablespoon black peppercorns

1 teaspoon crushed red pepper flakes

1 cinnamon stick, crushed

2 to 3 star anise pods

METHOD

1. Tightly layer the lemons, salt, and spices in a sturdy container with a tight-fitting lid. (I use a glass canning jar, but you can do this in Tupperware, too.) Be sure the lemons are completely covered with the salt and press them into the jar so that the lemons release their juice. Add more lemon juice or salt, as necessary, to completely submerge the fruit. Set aside at room temperature for 2 to 3 weeks. As they sit, the salt will liquefy and penetrate the lemons. Rinse the lemons and remove the seeds before chopping them up and adding them to recipes.

VARIATIONS

—**Purist.** Many cooks will scoff at my inclusion of spice. Pure salt and lemon is the classic, and to some, it is not a thing to be tampered with. I have no problem omitting the spices, if only to avoid the argument.

—**Other Citrus.** If you have an abundance of citrus of any kind, try preserving them in the same manner. You can experiment with the addition of herbs and spices if you dare. Limes look wonky after a while, as their bright green fades to avocado green. And depending on the thickness of the rind, the fruit may take longer to cure. But don't let that stop you! The flavor is no less amazing.

SNACKS AND HORS D'OEUVRES

The recipes in this chapter are entertainment-minded. These foods are historically presented at cocktail parties, or any special gathering that calls for more than a bag of Doritos. However, of all the chapters in this book, I probably turn to this one the most. That's because, since our kids grew and flew, our house sees far fewer formal meals. I like to think that we have morphed into a sort of tapas lifestyle. But really, we are just snacking our way through life in an empty nest. But don't feel sorry for us. These are damn good snacks.

These dishes are not groundbreaking or revolutionary. And I certainly can't claim ownership. (I am known for many things, but inventing pâté is not one of them.) But standard as they may be, they deserve a second look as a palate for artisan salt.

AVOCADO TOAST

Makes 2 toasts

I know you probably don't need a recipe for spreading delicious avocado on a slice of toast. It's pretty much a no-brainer. But it seems I can't open a food magazine or blog without reading about avocado toast, which makes me laugh, because I've been eating it since I was a kid. Often referred to as "poor man's butter," a good ripe avocado is actually more expensive than butter by weight for most of the year, in most of the country. So when you get a good one, treat it right.

INGREDIENTS

2 slices of your favorite bread, toasted (mine is whole grain sourdough)

1 large, perfectly ripe avocado

2 to 3 tablespoons extra-virgin olive oil

Zest and juice of ½ lemon

1 to 2 generous pinches of unrefined salt—*try Black Diamond, Murray River, Manzanillo, Mayan, a smoked salt, or a salt infused with lime, cumin, agave, chipotle, herbs, za'atar, or roasted garlic*

METHOD

1. Scoop out half the avocado onto each slice of toasted bread. With a fork, mash it into the grain, but not hard enough to smush the bread. Be sure to cover the entire surface of the bread with the avocado—all the way to the crust.

2. Grate the lemon zest over the avocado, then slice the lemon and squirt a bit of juice on top of the avocado. (I like only a little acid here, but feel free to use as much as you like.) Drizzle the olive oil over the top, and finish with a good pinch of salt. That's it. Simple perfection.

VARIATIONS

—**Put a Bird On It.** A fried, scrambled, or hard-boiled egg is the bomb on avocado toast. Sprinkle the salt on top of the egg. Add a little heat with sriracha sauce or chipotle salt . . . So good.

—**Herby Avo.** A generous pinch of chopped fresh herbs will brighten your "avo" toast. Try chives, chervil, or flat-leaf parsley, then sprinkle it with an herb-infused salt.

—**Cheese Avo.** Spread a dab of cream cheese on the toast first, for a creamier version. Or sprinkle the top with goat cheese. Or try melting some grated havarti on top, under the broiler, and add a sprinkle of a wine-infused salt on top!

—**Nutty Toast.** Sprinkle the top of your avocado toast with toasted pumpkin seeds, walnuts, pistachios, or Olive Oil–Roasted Almonds (page 89). Then finish with a smoked salt.

—**Garden Fresh.** Dice up a fresh tomato, and snip a few herbs straight from your garden. Or top with garlic-sautéed zucchini, asparagus, eggplant, or peppers. Then finish it off with a good pinch of roasted garlic or citrus salt.

CHICKEN LIVER PÂTÉ

Makes 4 to 6 servings

Much of the world finds nothing fancy about eating chicken livers. But somehow the French managed to elevate it (as they do with most mundane things—bread, underwear, cigarettes, words). You'll see what I mean. This recipe is a party staple, and I always make extra for morning-after snacks (a.k.a. breakfast). It can be made a day or two ahead, as the flavors improve as it sits.

INGREDIENTS

½ pound chicken livers, well cleaned (see sidebar)

2 shallots, chopped

3 to 4 sprigs fresh thyme

½ teaspoon unrefined salt—*try a sel gris, fleur de sel, Piran, Japanese shio, Maldon, a smoked salt, or a salt infused with herbs, red wine, cognac, port, anchovy, capers, fennel, seaweed, dashi, shiitake, or truffle*

¼ teaspoon freshly cracked black pepper

½ cup white wine

1 teaspoon cognac or brandy

12 tablespoons (1½ sticks/6 ounces) unsalted butter, at room temperature

2 tablespoons water

1 tablespoon powdered gelatin

¾ cup port wine or dry sherry

METHOD

1. Combine the livers, shallots, 1 sprig of thyme, salt, pepper, and wine in a small saucepan and bring to a simmer. Cook for 3 minutes, or until the livers are set and barely pink inside. Cover and set aside for 5 minutes.

2. Drain the liquid from the cooled livers, remove and discard the thyme sprigs, and transfer the solids to a food processor. Add the cognac and puree until smooth. Slowly add the butter, a tablespoon at a time, as the processor spins; this emulsifies and enriches the pâté. Transfer to a serving terrine, then spread and tap the top to smooth it. Place in the refrigerator.

3. Pour the water into a small bowl and sprinkle the gelatin on top. Set aside until the gelatin softens and absorbs the water, about 5 minutes. Bring the port and remaining thyme to a simmer. Add the gelatin and stir until it dissolves, then pour through a fine-mesh strainer onto the top of your pâté. Chill the pâté until set, at least an hour.

Serve with crackers, bread, cornichons, assorted pickles (see pages 66 and 67), onion jam (see page 95), sliced fresh radishes, or an assortment of cheese, fruits, and nuts.

VARIATION

—Jelly-free. If the idea of gelatin bums you out, you can finish your pâté with melted butter. Pour a very thin layer of hot melted butter on top of the chilled pâté. Before the butter sets, sprinkle the top with a solid layer of finely chopped parsley. Refrigerate until set, at least 30 minutes. Bring this version to room temperature for about 10 minutes before serving, so that the butter on top is not too brittle to spread nicely.

CLEANING LIVERS

Chicken livers are pretty cheap, as far as meat goes, but they do require a little attention before they can be cooked to their full potential. Wash them in cold water, then spread them out on a cutting board. Remove and discard the connective vein. Then pat the livers dry on a paper towel and continue with the recipe.

CARNE CRUDA

Makes about 4 servings

This is Italy's version of Beef Tartare. In Alba they add white truffles and it becomes *Carne all'albese*. You'll see that variation at the end. The key to good raw meat is threefold: good meat, cold meat, and a sharp knife.

INGREDIENTS

1 pound best-quality beef filet, well chilled

Finely grated zest and juice of 1 lemon

2 garlic cloves, halved

1 to 2 teaspoons unrefined salt—*try any fiore di sale, Murray River, Anglesey, Japanese shio, a smoked salt, a salt infused with truffle, anchovy, capers, seaweed, or serve it on a salt block*

Freshly ground black pepper

2 anchovy fillets, chopped

¼ to ½ cup extra-virgin olive oil

Sliced Italian bread or crackers

Lemon wedges, grated Parmesan cheese, cornichons (see Glossary page 199), or homemade pickles (see pages 66 and 67), for serving.

METHOD

1. Using your cleanest, sharpest knife, slice the meat into ¼-inch-thick strips, then into bâtons, then into ¼-inch dice. Then roughly chop until slightly smaller. Be careful not to create a meat paste. The finished chop should not resemble ground beef.

2. Place the chopped meat in a bowl. Add the lemon zest and juice, the garlic halves (you will retrieve these later), about ¾ teaspoon of the salt, pepper, and anchovy fillets. Mix well, then begin drizzling in the oil while stirring. The meat should just bind together. It should not look wet or greasy. Taste, then season again with additional salt and/or lemon as necessary.

3. Remove the garlic cloves, then divide the carne cruda among four plates. You can simply scoop it on, or press it into a nice shape using a ring mold, or whatever shape you like. Serve with sliced bread or crackers, and lemon wedges, grated Parmesan cheese, cornichons, or homemade pickles (see pages 66 and 67). You can also go the ultra umami route and garnish with shaved white or black truffles, chilled sautéed mushrooms, or more olive oil.

VARIATIONS

—**Salt Block Cruda.** This is one of my favorite things to serve on a salt block. Refrigerate your salt block overnight. Undersalt your meat (I usually reduce the salt to ¼ teaspoon) and serve as suggested, with the garnishes arranged on the block with the meat.

—**Carne Cruda all'albese.** Garnish with shaved white truffles.

OLIVE OIL–
ROASTED ALMONDS

POPCORN AND NUT
COCKTAIL MIX

GROWN-UP GORP

GROWN-UP GORP

Makes about 2 quarts gorp

Nuts and dried fruits have a very long relationship. From pemmican to Girl Scouts, they've always been perfectly matched. The sweet, spicy, salty additions in this recipe bring this classic trailside tradition into a modern urban setting.

INGREDIENTS

3 tablespoons brown sugar

2 teaspoons herbes de Provence

Grated zest of 1 orange

1¾ teaspoons unrefined salt—*try an American sea salt from the Pacific Northwest, Murray River, smoked salt, or a salt infused with orange, curry, paprika, saffron, chiles, or herbs*

½ to 1 teaspoon crushed red pepper flakes

1 cup pecan halves

1 cup whole skin-on almonds

1 cup cashews

1 cup hulled sunflower seeds

1 tablespoon sesame seed

1 tablespoon flaxseeds

1 tablespoon unsalted butter, melted

1 tablespoon honey

½ cup dried cherries or cranberries

½ cup pitted dates, chopped

½ cup golden raisins

¼ cup Zante currants

METHOD

1. Preheat the oven to 350°F. Coat a baking sheet with nonstick cooking spray and set aside. Mix together the sugar, herbs, orange zest, 1 teaspoon salt, and red pepper flakes. Set aside.

2. Toast the pecans, almonds, and cashews on dry baking sheets until golden and fragrant, about 10 minutes each. (I prefer to toast them separately.) Pour the hot nuts into a bowl, and add the sunflower, sesame, and flaxseeds. Add the butter and honey and toss to coat. Add the sugar mixture and continue to toss until evenly coated.

3. Spread the mixture out in an even layer on the prepared baking sheet. Bake in 5-minute increments, stirring in between, until the sugar has melted and the mixture is evenly toasted. Remove from the oven, toss with another ¾ teaspoon of salt, then cool completely.

4. When cool, add the cherries, dates, raisins, and currants. Toss together and serve, store airtight at room temperature for a week, or freeze for longer storage.

POPCORN AND NUT COCKTAIL MIX

Makes about 2 quarts cocktail mix

OK. I admit that this is basically dressed up Cracker Jacks. I just call it "cocktail mix" so it sounds more adult. But really, it's pretty darn good served with a Diet Coke.

INGREDIENTS

1 cup pecan halves

1 cup walnuts halves

1 cup peanuts

1 cup almonds

2 tablespoons unsalted butter

½ cup packed brown sugar

1½ teaspoons unrefined salt—*try Cyprus flake, Halen Môn, Hawaiian Popohaku, something from the American Pacific Northwest, a smoked salt, or a salt infused with maple, curry, bacon, sriracha, or orange*

Pinch of freshly ground black pepper

Pinch of ground white pepper

Pinch of crushed red pepper flakes

2 cups air-popped popcorn

METHOD

1. Preheat the oven to 350°F. Spread out the nuts on a dry baking sheet and toast for 5 to 10 minutes until golden and fragrant. (I like to do each nut separately.) Stir, then toast again for another 5 to 10 minutes. Keep warm.

2. Melt the butter in a large sauté pan over medium heat. Add the sugar, ½ teaspoon of the salt, the black and white peppers, and red pepper flakes and stir. Add the warm nuts, and toss over medium heat until the sugar has dissolved and the nuts are well coated. Add the popped popcorn, toss again, then immediately pour out on to a baking sheet. Stir in the remaining 1 teaspoon salt, then cool to room temperature before serving. Store airtight.

VARIATION

—Spice Options. Instead of the red pepper flakes, try the same recipe with a variety of spices and herbs. Rosemary is amazing when paired with grated orange zest. Thyme or sage work well with lemon zest. You can go the sweet route with cinnamon and nutmeg, or get exotic with some curry powder and a handful of dried figs or golden raisins.

FRIED GREEN ALMONDS

Makes 4 to 6 servings

My friend Kelly, whose family comes from Lebanon, turned me on to green almonds. Now I am hooked. She started me off by serving them raw with a simple sprinkle of good flake sea salt. Now I have graduated to a more involved preparation (although, not that much more involved). There is a short window of availability for these in the spring, so keep your eyes peeled. Be sure to choose young, green and fuzzy almonds, with gelatinous centers. (The fuzz is left on the young ones because it is very soft and tender.)

INGREDIENTS

2 cups young green almonds (no hard centers)

½ to 1 cup best-quality olive oil

Juice of ½ lemon

1 to 2 teaspoons unrefined salt—*try Persian Blue, Arabian fleur de sel, a Himalayan Pink, or a salt infused with ash, palm sugar, citrus, tea, paprika, or sriracha*

METHOD

1. Remove the almond stems with a paring knife, then rinse the almonds and pat dry.

2. Fill a large sauté pan with about ½ inch of oil and place over high heat. Test the oil's temperature by adding an almond. If the oil bubbles right away, it is ready (which will be 350 to 375°F). Add a handful of almonds (don't crowd them) and fry until they begin to turn golden, stirring frequently to get them as evenly colored as possible. Remove with a slotted spoon and drain on paper towels. Sprinkle with lemon juice and salt right away, while they are still hot, so it sticks. Serve immediately.

OLIVE OIL–ROASTED ALMONDS

Makes 2 cups roasted nuts

This is my favorite cocktail and wine-tasting accompaniment. My amazing friend Tina, who is a supertalented chef and artist, made this recipe for me once when she was hanging out at our place. I promptly stole it, and have passed it off as my own ever since. I think she's OK with that. She's pretty cool.

INGREDIENTS

2 cups whole, skin-on almonds

1 tablespoon extra-virgin olive oil

1 teaspoon unrefined salt—*try a Sicilian, Italian, or Spanish sea salt, a smoked salt, or an infused salt with herbs, roasted garlic, olives, kale, red wine, or curry*

2 tablespoons grated Parmesan cheese

¼ teaspoon dried thyme or herbes de Provence

METHOD

1. Preheat the oven to 350°F.

2. Spread the almonds out on a dry baking sheet and toast for 15 to 20 minutes until golden and fragrant. Stir every 5 minutes or so to ensure even browning.

3. Pour the hot nuts into a bowl, and add the oil and salt right away. Toss to coat, then add the cheese and herbs and toss again. Spread out again and cool to room temperature before serving. Store airtight.

KALE CHIPS

Makes about 4 cups chips

I know—kale has morphed from the "it-food" to the "hipster joke." But that's a little unfair. It has been around for a long time, and not just as an ornamental plant. You all know by now that dark greens are the good ones, so lay off the jokes, and make these fantastic chips. They are salty, crisp, and (gasp) healthy.

INGREDIENTS

1 pound curly kale, trimmed and torn into large but manageable bite-size pieces

1 tablespoon olive oil

1 teaspoon unrefined salt—*try Mali, Hana Flake, alaea, smoked, or a salt infused with fresh herbs, fennel, paprika, seaweed, dashi, tea, sesame*

METHOD

1. Preheat the oven to 350°F. Rinse and drain the kale leaves, and pat or spin dry. Transfer to a large bowl and toss with the oil and ½ teaspoon of the salt.

2. Arrange the leaves in a single layer on several baking sheets (you'll probably have to work in batches). Bake for 10 to 15 minutes, checking at the 5-minute mark to prevent burning (ovens vary—check for your own oven's hot spot). The leaves should still be green, but browned on the edges. They will crisp a little more after they cool.

3. As soon as they come out of the oven, sprinkle with the remaining ½ teaspoon salt. Cool completely, and serve. Store airtight at room temperature for a day or two.

VARIATION

—**Veggie Variations.** Try this same method to oven-fry thinly sliced root vegetables, such as beets, parsnips, or carrots. Use a mandolin to slice thin rounds, or a potato peeler for strips.

FRIED POTATO SKINS

KALE CHIPS

ZUCCHINI OVEN CHIPS

ZUCCHINI OVEN CHIPS

Makes 4 to 6 servings

I know zucchini oven chips sound like something your mom tried to trick you into eating—as if you wouldn't notice they weren't Ruffles. But if you know what you're getting into, they really do make a nice snack. And they are sure to impress all the sophisticated guests you've invited to your swanky cocktail party.

INGREDIENTS

¼ cup bread crumbs (I save bread ends and old crackers, then run them through the food processor)

¼ cup grated Parmesan cheese

1 teaspoon unrefined salt—*try a Northeast or Gulf Coast sea salt, or a salt infused with herbs, roasted garlic, anchovy, shiitake, beer, tea, or chiles*

⅓ teaspoon dried oregano

⅓ teaspoon freshly ground black pepper

1 garlic clove, minced

½ cup whole milk

4 large zucchini, sliced into ⅓-inch-thick wheels

METHOD

1. Preheat the oven to 425°F. Line a baking sheet with a wire rack, then coat the rack with nonstick cooking spray.

2. In a small bowl, mix together the crumbs, cheese, ½ teaspoon of the salt, oregano, and pepper. In a separate small bowl, stir together minced garlic and milk.

3. Dip each zucchini slice into the garlicky milk, then coat each side generously with the crumb mixture. Place close together on the prepared rack in a single layer. Bake for 30 to 45 minutes until browned and crisp. Rotate the pan for even cooking.

4. As soon as the zucchini are out of the oven, sprinkle with the remaining salt. Serve hot as is, or with a dipping sauce, like Creamy Buttermilk Dressing (page 128).

FRIED POTATO SKINS

Makes 4 to 6 servings

The first time I had potato skins was at T.G.I. Fridays, and we thought it was crazy! When it opened, it was an amazing place for teenagers. There was really nothing like it in the early 1980s. Now, there are thousands of places just like it. Using potato skins in this way was first an exercise in frugality—finding a use for literal garbage. But more often than not, I find myself having to manufacture uses for the potato insides. If you make these first, freeze the potato insides for a later date.

INGREDIENTS

4 russet potatoes

1 to 2 cups peanut or canola oil

1 to 2 teaspoons unrefined sea salt—*try Murray River, Hana Flake, an American salt from the Northeast, a charcoal-infused black salt, a smoked salt, or a salt infused with bacon, anchovy, curry, peppercorns, roasted garlic, or sriracha*

METHOD

1. Heat about 2 inches of oil in a heavy, high-sided pot until it reaches 350 to 375°F. Peel off the potato skins lengthwise, and with a generous amount of potato attached. (Find a peeler that takes off thick strips, or use a paring knife). Do not let the potato strips sit around too long, or they will oxidize to an unattractive (but harmless) gray color.

2. Drop the potato skins, by the handful, into the hot oil. Cook, stirring carefully, until golden on all sides. Using a spider (see Glossary page 203), or a slotted spoon, remove the fried potato strips from the oil and drain on paper towels. Salt while still hot and wet, then repeat to cook the remaining potato strips. Serve immediately with your favorite condiment. The traditional TGIF treatment included sour cream, grated cheese, bacon bits, and chives. I am partial to Pasilla Aioli (page 134).

VARIATION

—Root Options. Use sweet potatoes, yams, purple Peruvian potatoes, fingerlings, or any other cool potato. Or try the same method with carrots and parsnips. It sounds healthy, but never fear—it is still fried in oil.

SWEET POTATO CHIPS

RED BEET CHIPS

GOLDEN BEET CHIPS

BEETS AND SWEETS

Makes enough for 4 snackers

Taking a cue from the mouth explosion that is sweet and salt, there are few things that make better salty chips than the sweet roots. This combo is particularly savory, and beautiful. I like making these just to set around the house decoratively. Of course, they don't last long when I do.

INGREDIENTS

1 to 2 cups peanut or canola oil, for frying

2 large sweet potatoes or yams, washed and dried

2 large beets, washed and dried

2 to 3 teaspoons unrefined salt—*try a flor de sal, Saltverk, Sal de Maras, a smoked salt, or a salt infused with agave, bacon, horseradish, mustard, anise, sweet spice, or sesame*

METHOD

1. Heat about 2 inches of oil in a heavy, high-sided pot until it reaches 350 to 375°F.

2. Slice the sweet potatoes and beets about ⅓ inch thick, using a mandoline or a very sharp knife. When the oil is hot, add a handful of the slices to the oil. (Add them carefully, and don't crowd the pot.) Cook, stirring occasionally, until they begin to turn golden, and the oil stops bubbling. The beets will shrink and curl at the edges when they're ready. Using a spider or a slotted spoon, remove the chips from the oil and drain on paper towels. Salt while they're still hot and wet, then repeat to cook the remaining chips. Serve immediately.

VARIATION

—Roots. Try this recipe with other roots, like yucca, parsnip, purple potatoes, or regular potatoes. You can't go wrong.

ONION JAM ALLUMETTES

Makes about 2 dozen pastries

Allumette is the classic French culinary term for strips of puff pastry. The word means "matchstick," but these are certainly not meant to be that thin. Aim for creating bite-size rectangles.

INGREDIENTS

¼ cup olive oil

2½ pounds red onions, peeled, halved, and thinly sliced

1 to 2 teaspoons unrefined salt—*try Halen Môn, flor de sal, a smoked salt, or a salt infused with fresh herbs, roasted garlic, capers, anchovy, olives, seaweed, chipotle, shiitake, or truffle*

¼ teaspoon freshly ground black pepper

2 bay leaves

2 sprigs fresh thyme

¼ cup granulated sugar

⅓ cup dry white wine

⅓ red wine vinegar

1 egg

1 tablespoon water

1 package frozen puff pastry, defrosted in the refrigerator overnight

METHOD

1. Heat the oil in a large, heavy skillet over high heat. Add the onions, reduce the heat, and cook, stirring, for 5 minutes, until the onions begin to sweat and soften. Cover the pan and cook, stirring occasionally, over low heat until they begin to color, about 30 minutes.

MELON AND SALT WITH HONEY MINT PESTO

Makes 2 to 4 servings

Salted melon is an old-timey snack. There is some version of it in most cultures. My grandmother used to tell me it made the melon sweeter, which I always suspected was just crazy talk. It does, however, get your taste buds firing on all cylinders, which is pretty awesome. There are a hundred variations of this dish, and I'm sure you can probably think of your own. The point is to take full advantage of the sweet-salt pairing. It's one of my favorites. You can serve this as a salad, too, or on a chilled salt block, which is the most fun presentation ever.

INGREDIENTS

About 4 cups assorted ripe melons, diced into 1-inch cubes

2 cups fresh mint leaves

½ cup fresh tarragon leaves

1 teaspoon peeled and grated fresh ginger

1¼ cups honey

Grated zest and juice of ½ lemon

1 teaspoon unrefined salt—try *Maldon, Mali, Manzanillo, Black Diamond, or a salt infused with chiles, lime, pink peppercorns, Li Hing Mui, date sugar, or ginger*

Pinch of freshly cracked pepper

1 to 2 tablespoons olive oil

METHOD

1. Cut the melon into decorative but uniform pieces and set aside in the refrigerator to chill.

2. Wash the mint and tarragon leaves and combine them in a blender with the ginger, honey, lemon zest, and ½ teaspoon of the salt. Process to a rough chop, then drizzle the oil in slowly, blending until the paste is silky and smooth. You may need to add additional water, drop by drop, to achieve this texture. Finish with the lemon juice, adding a little at a time to achieve a balanced flavor.

3. Arrange melon on a platter, or on skewers. Sprinkle with remaining ½ teaspoon salt, pepper, then drizzle with the herb paste. If you serve this on a salt block, omit the last ½ teaspoon of salt on top of the melon. The seasoning will come from underneath!

VARIATIONS

—Cheesy. A creamy crumble of goat, ricotta, or handmade farmer's cheese (page 61) adds a great textural balance to the crispy cool melon.

—Exotic. Replace the herb paste in this recipe with Harissa (page 130), or drizzle the melon with yogurt and sprinkle with chopped fresh cilantro and Kala Namak salt.

SOUPS AND SALADS

As a Southern California resident, I typically serve more salad than soup. One reason for this is that it's hardly ever soup weather here. Another is that I have one kid that historically refused it. She couldn't wrap her head around the idea of a savory liquid. In her mind, liquid is for beverages, not dinner. I'm not sure where this phobia came from, but she's a college graduate now, and still won't touch the stuff. Rest assured, when she moved out, I brought the soup pot out of storage.

Though often used as the first course, these recipes hold their own at lunch, for a light dinner, and as side dishes. And though some may seem familiar, the use of artisanal salt will bring out elements of flavor and texture that will make them fresh and new.

AJO BLANCO (WHITE GAZPACHO)

Makes 3 to 4 servings

In the States, we typically think of gazpacho as a cold red tomato soup. But the original Andalusian soup comes in many colors. This garlicky white soup is probably close to the original, bread-thickened version brought to the region by Arabs. Like most stale bread recipes, it doesn't work as well with the fresh stuff. The moisture needs to leave the bread, so there is room for the flavorful moisture you're adding in the form of sherry, olive oil, garlic, etc.

INGREDIENTS

½ cup golden raisins or dried figs (or a bit of each)

1 cup boiling water

1 cup dry Spanish sherry (try a Fino or dry Oloroso, then drink it with your soup, too)

½ cup whole milk

3 cups stale French or sourdough bread, crusts removed, torn into bite-size pieces

1 cup whole, skin-on almonds

3 garlic cloves

½ cup green grapes

1 teaspoon unrefined salt—*try Spanish or Portuguese flor de sal, Mali, Atlas, or a salt infused with almond, roasted garlic, date sugar, sherry, paprika, or chiles*

¼ cup extra virgin olive oil, plus more for drizzling

METHOD

1. Combine the raisins (or figs) and water, and set aside to plump for 30 minutes. (You can do this with cold water overnight if you have the forethought.)

2. In a large bowl, pour the raisin water, sherry, and milk over the bread, and set aside to soak and soften for 30 to 60 minutes.

3. Roughly chop the almonds in a food processor. Set a couple of tablespoons aside to garnish the finished dish. Add the garlic and continue to process to a fine paste. Add the plumped raisins, grapes, ½ teaspoon of the salt and continue to process. Squeeze the excess liquid from the bread, but reserve it. Add the bread to the processor and continue blending, adding the bread liquid as needed to facilitate a smooth, souplike texture. Finally, slowly pour in the ¼ cup of olive oil.

4. Pass the soup through a fine-mesh strainer, and season again with additional salt as needed. Chill the soup for at least an hour (or overnight).

5. Divide the soup among chilled bowls, then garnish with an additional drizzle of oil, the reserved chopped almonds, and another small pinch of salt.

GREEN GAZPACHO

Makes 3 to 4 servings

Another alternative to the cold red tomato soup is this herby green version. It is thickened with bread like its white cousin, but has a fresher, brighter flavor. If you are looking for the red version, see the variations below.

INGREDIENTS

2 to 3 cups diced French or Italian-style bread, crust removed

¼ cup sherry vinegar

Grated zest and juice of 1 lemon, plus more juice as needed

1 cup buttermilk or sour cream

2 tomatillos, husked and roughly chopped

½ cup chopped almonds, toasted and kept warm

4 English or Persian cucumbers

1 large Anaheim chile, fire-roasted

2 scallions, chopped, plus more for garnish

2 garlic cloves

1 teaspoon unrefined salt—try Spanish or Portugese flor de sal, Manzanillo, Mayan, Sal de Maras, or a salt infused with chile, cumin, almond, lime, onion, sherry, peppercorns, or cilantro

1 cup watercress or spinach leaves

1 cup fresh cilantro leaves

1 teaspoon ground cumin

½ teaspoon ground coriander

½ teaspoon freshly ground black pepper

1 ripe avocado, pitted, peeled, and diced

Sour cream, for serving

Crusty French bread, for serving

METHOD

1. In a large bowl, combine the bread with the sherry vinegar, lemon zest and juice, buttermilk, and tomatillos. Set aside for 30 minutes to soak.

2. In a blender, pulverize the warm almonds as finely as you can. Add the cucumbers, chile, scallions, garlic, and ½ teaspoon of the salt. Pulse to create a chunky puree. Add the watercress, cilantro, and cumin, coriander, and pepper. Continue to puree, adding cold water by tablespoons as needed to achieve a smooth soup consistency. Pass the soup through a fine-mesh strainer, and chill for at least 30 minutes, or overnight.

3. Just before serving, puree again with the avocado to create a thick soup consistency. Season again with salt and lemon juice as needed. Pour into chilled soup bowls and garnish with chopped scallions, a dollop of sour cream, and another pinch of salt. Serve with crusty French bread.

VARIATIONS

—Red Gazpacho. Replace the tomatillos and cucumber with super-ripe red tomatoes, and add 1 to 2 roasted red bell peppers (homemade or store-bought) in place of the Anaheim chile. Omit the watercress and avocado, and try a pinch of smoked salt.

—Yellow Gazpacho. Replace the tomatillos and cucumber with super-ripe yellow tomatoes, and add 1 to 2 roasted yellow or orange bell peppers in place of the Anaheim chile. Omit the watercress, and use the cilantro and avocado only as garnish. Try this with a pinch of Murray River, or a spicy sriracha salt.

KABOCHA SQUASH SOUP WITH HAZELNUTS

Makes 4 to 6 servings

My favorite part of autumn is the culinary permission I get to cook with winter squashes. Pumpkin, butternut, acorn, and my favorite, the kabocha, make their way into side dishes, desserts, salads, and lots of great soup. Feel free to use your favorite winter squash here, and your favorite nut, for that matter. See the variations below for some classic combos.

INGREDIENTS

1 small kabocha squash

¼ to ½ cup olive oil

1 teaspoon unrefined salt—*try a sel gris, Japanese shio, Pangasinan Star, or a salt infused with garlic, orange, sage, sherry, or hazelnuts*

6 to 8 garlic cloves, peeled

½ large yellow onion

¼ cup hazelnuts

1 to 2 cups vegetable broth, chicken broth, or water

1 cup half-and-half

6 to 8 large fried fresh sage leaves

METHOD

1. Preheat the oven to 400°F. Cut the squash into quarters and scoop out the seeds. Coat the interior with olive oil and sprinkle with salt. Set the squash on a baking sheet, cut side up, and roast until tender, about 1 hour.

2. Meanwhile, place the garlic cloves in a piece of aluminum foil, drizzle with oil, and wrap tightly. Roast in the same oven until tender, about 30 minutes. Peel the onion and cut into 6 to 8 wedges, keeping the root ends intact. Place on a baking sheet, drizzle with oil, and roast in the same oven until browned and tender, about 30 minutes.

3. Spread out the hazelnuts on a dry baking sheet and toast in the same oven until fragrant and browned, about 5 minutes. When each element is cooked as directed, set aside until cool.

4. Roughly chop the cooled nuts with a pinch of salt, then set aside for the garnish.

5. Scoop the squash pulp out of its skin, and put into a blender along with the roasted garlic. Slice the root end off of each roasted onion quarter, and add the onions to the blender. Puree until smooth, adding broth or water as necessary to facilitate blending, but not too much—it should be a thick soup consistency.

6. Pass the puree through a fine-mesh strainer into a saucepan. Warm gently over medium heat. Add the half-and-half, taste, and season with more salt as necessary. Keep the soup warm.

7. Heat 2 to 3 tablespoons of olive oil in a small sauté pan. When hot, add the sage leaves, and fry until the sizzling stops and they are crisp and toasted, about 20 seconds. Drain on paper towels.

8. Serve the soup warm, with a sprinkle of chopped hazelnuts and a couple of fried sage leaves.

VARIATIONS

—Pumpkin. Try this recipe using pumpkin, and garnish with toasted pepitas (a.k.a. pumpkin seeds).

—Italianate. Use butternut squash, and add a tablespoon or two of chopped fresh rosemary to the roasting pan. Garnish with grated Parmesan cheese, toasted almonds, or crumbled amaretti cookies.

PURPLE VICHYSSOISE

Makes 4 to 6 servings

I like to cook to the beat of my own drummer. I have been enamored with purple potatoes ever since I first saw them twenty years ago. They have a flavor slightly sweeter than a red potato, but not as sweet as a purple yam. They can be used for just about any potato preparation, and are more fun simply because they are purple. Nothin' wrong with a little random fun.

INGREDIENTS

1 tablespoon unsalted butter

½ cup chopped purple onion

¼ cup chopped celery

½ teaspoon herbes de Provence

3 cups purple potatoes, peeled and roughly sliced

2 cups water

1 teaspoon unrefined salt—*try Mali, Peruvian Pink, or a salt infused with lavender, thyme, lemon, tea, or pink peppercorns*

1 tablespoon fresh lemon juice

1 cup half-and-half

Pinch of freshly ground white pepper

2 tablespoons browned butter, for garnish

1 teaspoon dried lavender buds, for garnish

METHOD

1. In a large sauté pan, combine the butter with the onion, celery, and herbs. Cook for 1 to 2 minutes until the butter has melted and the vegetables are tender. Add the potatoes, water, and ½ teaspoon of the salt and simmer on medium heat until the potatoes are tender, 20 to 30 minutes. Remove from the heat and cool.

2. Drain off the excess liquid and reserve. Transfer the contents to a blender and puree until smooth, adding cooking liquid as needed to achieve a soup consistency. Pass the soup through a fine-mesh strainer and cool completely.

3. Just before serving, stir in the lemon juice, half-and-half, pepper, and more salt as needed.

4. Divide the soup among serving bowls and garnish each with a drizzle of browned butter, a pinch more of salt, and a pinch of lavender.

VARIATIONS

—Cheesy. This soup is terrific garnished with a crumble of soft, fresh cheese. Try goat, ricotta, or a homemade Farmer's Cheese (page 61).

—Baconssoise. Vichyssoise is often made with bacon instead of butter. Add 1 slice of bacon with the onion, celery, and herbs and cook until it is crisp. Remove and reserve the crisp bacon, drain off the excess fat, and continue with the recipe. When serving, garnish with the crumbled bacon.

—Traditional. Make the original Vichyssoise (which gets its name from the town of Vichy, whose therapeutic waters were swam in, drunk, and added to all kinds of dishes) by using russet potatoes instead of the purple ones, leeks instead of the purple onion, and thyme instead of the herbes de Provence. Salt for the classic version should be *sel gris, fleur de sel, Halen Môn, Black Diamond, or a salt infused with thyme, lemon, fennel, roasted garlic, celery salt, saffron, or truffle.*

PURPLE VICHYSSOISE

SUMMER MELON SOUP

Makes 4 to 6 servings

In the 1980s I saw melon soup on dessert menus fairly frequently. I always thought it was a cheap shortcut by lazy chefs. But lately I have had a change of heart, and have come to appreciate melon soup for its refreshing quality. I'd rather see it as an appetizer or a palate-cleansing course than a dessert, but I no longer turn up my nose, wherever it appears. Here I have paired it with salty meats, but look to the variations for some dessert ideas.

INGREDIENTS

1 large yellow, orange, or green melon (try a Hami, Sharlyn, Crenshaw, or honeydew)

½ cup honey

5 to 6 fresh mint leaves

1 teaspoon peeled and grated fresh ginger

Grated zest of 1 orange

½ cup champagne or orange juice

1 teaspoon unrefined salt—*try fiore di sale, Mayan, Pangasinan Star, or a salt infused with mint, ginger, curry, Li Hing Mui, sweet spices, tea, or Szechuan pepper*

¼ cup fresh lime juice, or more as needed

½ cup plain Greek yogurt or Farmer's Cheese (page 61)

8 slices thinly shaved prosciutto, ham, or Basturma (page 62)

METHOD

1. Peel and seed the melon and combine it in a blender with the honey, mint leaves, ginger, orange zest, and champagne. Puree until very smooth, then add ½ teaspoon of the salt and the lime juice. Chill for at least 30 minutes.

2. Before serving, taste again and adjust the seasoning with more salt and lime juice as needed. As the melon soup chills, it will probably separate, but don't be alarmed. Simply give it a stir just before serving in chilled bowls, garnished with yogurt, shaved prosciutto, and a few melon balls of a contrasting color.

VARIATIONS

—Spicy. Add freshly ground black or pink peppercorns, or even a dash of sriracha, for a refreshingly zingy variation.

—Thick and Creamy. A heartier, more savory version of this soup can be made by omitting the honey and mint, and adding a brick of silken tofu, a chopped scallion, and a dash of soy sauce to the blender. Garnish with toasted sesame seeds and a pinch of wakame or dashi salt.

—Desserty. Garnish this soup with a scoop of vanilla ice cream or fruity sorbet, and a delicate Crisp Salty Meringue (page 197).

CARDAMOM CURRIED CAULIFLOWER AND LENTIL SOUP

Makes 3 to 4 servings

Cardamom is my favorite spice of all time. It is equally at home in curry as it is in a coffee cake. But ground cardamom is not always of the highest quality. If you have the choice, buy whole cardamom pods, either green or black. To use, open the outer hull, remove the seeds, and crush them in a mortar with a pestle or in a coffee mill.

INGREDIENTS

1 tablespoon coconut oil, ghee, or butter

4 large cardamom pods, hulled, seeds crushed

½ teaspoon cumin seeds

½ cinnamon stick

3 scallions, chopped

3 garlic cloves

1 teaspoon garam masala

½ head cauliflower, separated into small florets (about 2 cups)

1 cup lentils

4 cups vegetable broth or water

One 15-ounce can chickpeas, with their liquid

1 teaspoon unrefined salt—*try Mali, Atlas, Arabian fleur de sel, Kala Namak, or a salt infused with bahārāt (see Glossary), cardamom, lemon, curry, cumin, palm sugar, roasted garlic, ginger, or sesame*

1 cup paneer or plain yogurt, for serving

Quickest Cucumber Pickles (page 66) or Raita (page 137), for serving (optional)

METHOD

1. In a large saucepan over medium-high heat, heat the coconut oil. Add the cardamom, cumin, and cinnamon, and toast until fragrant, about 1 minute. Reduce the heat to medium, add the scallions and garlic, and cook until tender. Stir in the garam masala.

2. Add the cauliflower florets and cook for 3 to 5 minutes, stirring to coat with spices. Add the lentils and broth, and cook over medium heat, stirring occasionally, until tender, about 30 minutes. Add the chickpeas and their liquid, and cook until warmed through. Season with more salt as needed. Remove and discard the cinnamon stick.

3. Serve over rice, topped with another pinch of salt, a dollop of yogurt, and a side of Quickest Cucumber Pickles (page 66) or Raita (page 137), if you like.

VARIATIONS

—Cukes. Thin slices of Persian cucumbers are a logical addition. You can also add some quick-cured cucumber pickles for a welcome zippy tang (see page 66).

—Spicy Greens. The peppery hint of watercress or arugula play nicely off the cool dill dressing. Add in equal proportion to the butter lettuce.

—Canapés. A small pile of this salad, nested on top of brioche or pumpernickel toast points and topped with a thin smear of soft cheese, makes an amazing cocktail treat.

BUTTER LETTUCE AND RADISH SLAW

Makes 2 to 4 servings

I am a huge coleslaw fan, and have routinely been caught eating it for breakfast (usually on the morning after a rowdy BBQ). This version is a twist on the traditional French butter and radish sandwich. You can eat it as is, or scoop it up with a hunk of buttered baguette for the full effect. It is a great recipe to use when fancy radishes hit the market.

INGREDIENTS

1 small head butter lettuce

5 to 6 large radishes

¼ cup fresh flat-leaf parsley leaves

¼ cup chopped fresh chives or scallions

Finely grated zest and juice of ½ lemon

1 tablespoon olive oil

1 tablespoon honey

1 teaspoon dried dill

1 teaspoon unrefined salt—*try any fleur de sel, or Maldon, Hana Flake, Black Diamond, or a salt infused with chive, dill, lemon, celery salt, lavender, or pink peppercorns*

METHOD

1. Cut the lettuce into thin ribbons (known in the biz as a *chiffonade;* see Glossary page 199). Trim and slice the radishes into very thin matchsticks or rounds. Combine in a salad bowl with the lettuce, parsley, and chives.

2. In a smaller bowl, whisk together the lemon zest and juice, olive oil, honey, dill, and ½ teaspoon of the salt. Drizzle enough of the dressing into the salad bowl to lightly but thoroughly coat the slaw. Refrigerate for 30 minutes. Just before serving sprinkle with another pinch of the salt.

GRILLED GREENS SALAD

Makes 4 to 6 servings

I love grilling food—any food. Nothing is spared the rack, including salad. The smoky char, available only from an open fire, is the secret ingredient in many of my dishes. Shhhh. Oh, wait . . . Shoot.

INGREDIENTS

4 heads Belgian endive

2 large heads romaine, loose outer leaves removed (or purchase romaine hearts)

1 head frisée

1 purple onion, peeled and quartered, root ends intact

2 to 3 tablespoons olive oil

Juice of ½ lemon

1 teaspoon unrefined salt—*try fiore di sale, Anglesey, Bali Pyramid, Black Diamond, a smoked salt, or a salt infused with agave, lemon, kale, hazelnut, paprika, pesto, shiitake, red wine, or balsamic vinegar*

¼ cup fresh flat-leaf parsley leaves, minced

METHOD

1. Preheat a grill on high. Combine the whole lettuce heads and onion in a large bowl with 1 tablespoon of the oil and toss to coat. Place them on the grill and cook, turning frequently, until well charred on all sides.

2. Transfer to a cutting board, slice the heads lengthwise at the roots (into halves or quarters, depending on the size) and return to the bowl. Slice the root end off the onion quarters and add the onions to the bowl. Add the lemon juice, ½ teaspoon of the salt, and more oil as needed. Toss and serve while still warm, topped with a sprinkle of parsley and a final pinch of the salt.

VARIATION

—Go Green. You can make this salad with any of your favorite greens. Try to have an assortment of mild and bitter greens, so the entire dish is balanced. Consider adding Swiss chard, kale, arugula, radicchio, spinach, or butter lettuce.

BURST CHERRY TOMATO SALAD

Makes 4 to 6 servings

This recipe is great as a side dish, poured on top of pasta or polenta, stirred into risotto, spread warm over toast, or chilled and spread on your hamburgers. It's best if the tomatoes come from your garden. But if you have a black thumb (like me), good-quality, perfectly ripe market tomatoes work just as well.

INGREDIENTS

¼ cup olive oil

4 cups cherry tomatoes (choose assorted colors if you can)

1 teaspoon unrefined salt—try *Halen Môn, Murray River, fiore di sale, Black Lava, smoked salt, or a salt infused with chipotle, fennel seed, balsamic vinegar, basil, pesto, peppercorns, roasted garlic, or red wine*

2 garlic cloves, sliced

Grated zest and juice of 1 lemon

METHOD

1. Heat 3 tablespoons of the oil in a large sauté pan over high heat. Add one-third of the tomatoes and cook, shaking gently, until they start to break their skin, about 5 minutes. Reduce the heat to medium and add another third of the tomatoes and ½ teaspoon of the salt. Continue to cook, shaking and stirring, for another 3 to 4 minutes until tomatoes burst. Transfer the tomatoes to a dish, and return the pan to the heat.

2. Add the remaining 1 tablespoon oil to the pan, then add the garlic. Cook, stirring, until the garlic softens, about 1 minute. Add the remaining raw tomatoes and the reserved cooked tomatoes, and cook, stirring, until the last batch of tomatoes begins to burst. The mixture should be juicy and thick, with a variety of tomato textures. Remove from the heat and season with the lemon juice and more salt as needed. Serve warm, at room temperature, or cold.

VARIATIONS

—Balsamic Tomatoes. Finish this dish with 2 tablespoons of balsamic vinegar instead of the lemon juice, add a handful of basil leaves, cut into chiffonade, and finish with a grating of fresh Parmesan or some diced buffalo mozzarella.

—Fennel Tomatoes. Before you burst the tomatoes, sauté a sliced fennel bulb in the olive oil with a pinch of salt and a teaspoon of toasted and crushed fennel seeds. Remove it from the pan, then stir it back into the mix when the tomatoes are done. Garnish with some reserved fennel fronds.

BURST CHERRY
TOMATO SALAD

SWEET PEA AND SPRING VEGETABLES SALAD

Makes 4 to 6 servings

Fresh peas are one of my favorite spring things, but this recipe can easily be made year-round with any vegetable that is in season. And, by the way, fresh frozen peas are usually pretty high quality. See the variations for some ideas.

INGREDIENTS

½ red onion, diced

2 cups thin asparagus

2 cups baby spring squash (zucchini, yellow, patty pan, whatever is fresh)

1 cup squash blossoms, chopped roughly

2 cups fresh sweet peas

2 cups snow peas

1 cup thinly sliced radishes

¼ cup fresh mint leaves, chopped

1 teaspoon unrefined salt—*try Anglesey, Cyprus flake, Maldon, Black Diamond, or a salt infused with citrus, ginger, kale, capers, bacon, anchovy, mint, peppercorns, or mixed herbs*

Finely grated zest and juice of 1 lemon

¼ cup extra-virgin olive oil

¼ cup toasted and chopped pistachios

METHOD

1. Place the diced onion in a bowl of cold water and set aside for at least 10 minutes. This helps remove some of the harsh volatile oils that make your breath stinky. Fill another large bowl with ice water and set aside.

2. Bring a medium pot of water to a boil, and blanch the asparagus and squash separately for 20 to 30 seconds each, until they are brightly colored. Using a slotted spoon, immediately transfer them to the ice water, cool, and drain.

3. In a large bowl, combine the squash blossoms, peas, snow peas, radishes, mint, drained diced onion, and cooled blanched vegetables. Add ½ teaspoon of the salt and toss together gently. In a separate small bowl, combine the lemon zest, lemon juice, and oil. Stir, then add as much dressing as needed to thoroughly—but not overly—coat the vegetables. To serve, top the salad with the toasted pistachios and another pinch of the salt.

VARIATIONS

—Winter Mix. Try this dish with Brussels sprouts and cauliflower instead of the spring veggies. Blanch, chop, and mix them with grated carrots, parsnips, and celery root. Add some fresh chopped dill in place of the mint.

—Creamy. Make a creamy dressing by adding ¼ cup of buttermilk or sour cream to the lemon and oil.

AVOCADO-GRAPEFRUIT SALT BLOCK SALAD

Makes 2 to 4 servings

While it is possible to cook on a salt block, by far my favorite use for it is the presentation of food. The surface does the salting, and the way the salt rises from underneath the dish is a palate-pleaser. This is one of my favorites. See the variations for some other salty combos.

INGREDIENTS

8–12" square or rectangular salt block

1 grapefruit, peeled and cut into segments (suprêmes)

1 avocado, sliced

1 tablespoon olive oil

¼ teaspoon freshly ground pink or black peppercorns

METHOD

1. Arrange the grapefruit suprêmes and avocado slices alternately across a clean, chilled salt block. Drizzle with the olive oil and sprinkle with the ground peppercorns. Set aside at room temperature for 10 minutes before serving, to allow the salt to penetrate. If the day is particularly hot, chill the entire block for 30 minutes for a more refreshing course.

VARIATIONS

—No Salt Block. Make the same dish on a plate, and finish with a generous pinch of Himalayan, Black Diamond, any sel gris, a smoked salt, or a salt infused with citrus, chiles, cilantro, chocolate, peppercorns, or Mexican sweet chili salt

—Cucumber, Avocado, and Tomato. For a more savory salt block salad, replace the grapefruit with slices of cucumber and tomato. A little chiffonade of basil, or some fresh dill would be a nice addition here.

—Salty Caprese. The classic caprese salad of tomato, buffalo mozzarella, and basil is given a new lease on life when served on a salt block. Drizzle with olive oil and a little balsamic vinegar.

FORBIDDEN RICE SALAD

Makes 4 to 6 servings

Chinese black rice is a nutrient-rich, nutty, heirloom rice that is actually a deep purple. They say that, historically, it was reserved for emperors. I'm skeptical, though. If all the foods that make that claim really were just for emperors, those emperors would have been really fat. You can vary the vegetables in this dish to fit the season, or switch it up to reflect another cuisine. See the variations for ideas.

INGREDIENTS

1 tablespoon vegetable oil

8 to 10 baby bok choy

½ teaspoon sesame oil

½ purple onion, diced

1 celery stalk, thinly sliced on the bias

2 garlic cloves, minced

One 1-inch piece fresh ginger, peeled and grated

1 cup garlic chives or regular chives, cut in 2-inch length

1 teaspoon sesame seeds

2 tablespoons rice vinegar

Finely grated zest and juice of 1 lime

1 cup cooked black rice, cooled

1 teaspoon unrefined salt—*try a Japanese shio, Sogum, Pangasinan Star, bamboo, smoked salt, or a salt infused with citrus, kale, roasted garlic, sesame, seaweed, soy sauce, tea, or ginger*

METHOD

1. Heat the vegetable oil in a large wok or sauté pan over high heat. Add the bok choy and cook briefly, until charred and wilted, about 5 minutes. Remove the bok choy and set aside.

2. To the same pan, add the sesame oil, onions, celery, garlic, and ginger. Cook on medium heat until wilted. Add the garlic chives and sesame seeds and cook another minute, until the seeds start to toast. Add the vinegar and lime zest and juice, and remove from the heat. Return the bok choy to the pan, add the rice, and ½ teaspoon of the salt. Toss everything until well coated, then refrigerate until chilled completely. Serve with a final sprinkle of the salt.

VARIATIONS

—**Grain Options.** I love the look of black rice, but there are many other grains that would be just as scrumptious in this recipe. Try quinoa, millet, kamut, jasmine rice, or everyday brown rice.

—**Veggie Options.** This salad has obvious Asian overtones, but you can add any vegetable you see fit to it. In fact, using what you have on hand, or choosing what is good in the market, is exactly what a good emperor should do.

MARINATED SMOKED TOFU SALAD

Makes 4 to 6 servings

I first had this dish marinated in liquid smoke, which I do not particularly like. (Liquid smoke tastes too manufactured to me.) But when I discovered smoked salt, all the liquid smoke recipes I have been avoiding were suddenly accessible. This is a terrific one, especially if you are in search of something new to feed your vegetarian friends. I have put it in a salad here, but it makes a great sandwich and canapé element, too.

INGREDIENTS

One 12-ounce package extra-firm tofu

2 tablespoons olive oil

1 tablespoon smoked salt

Finely grated zest and juice of ½ lemon

3 cups mixed greens

1 pint cherry tomatoes, halved

¼ cup fresh flat-leaf parsley leaves, minced, plus extra for garnish

¼ cup toasted sliced almonds

METHOD

1. Unwrap the tofu and sandwich it between two plates. Weigh down the top with something like a soup can or a tub of sour cream and refrigerate for 30 to 60 minutes. This forces out excess moisture, and makes the tofu easier to slice.

2. Cut the pressed tofu into ½-inch slices and pack them in a small container with alternating layers of smoked salt and olive oil. Cover and refrigerate for 6 hours, or overnight.

3. Transfer the tofu to a large bowl, oil and all. Add the lemon zest and juice, mixed greens, cherry tomatoes, parsley, and almonds. Toss to coat, then divide evenly among serving plates. Garnish with parsley and a final pinch of smoked salt.

VARIATIONS

—**Tomato Tofu.** Dice the marinated tofu and toss it with diced fresh tomatoes and chopped grilled scallions.

—**Tofu Pickles.** Dice the smoked tofu and toss it with the pickled vegetables from page 65. Serve on top of greens, or as a tangy side dish.

SAUCES, CONDIMENTS, AND DRESSINGS

I t's easy to salt a dish. But seasoning with a salty condiment, sauce, or dressing takes your cooking to another level. Think outside the box (of salt), and give some of these food accessories a try.

I have included a small handful of chutney recipes here, because I think there are few toppings that excite your cooking quite the way chutney does. There are literally hundreds of chutney recipes, all from different regions of South Asia. Try these, then venture out on your own chutney quest.

There are a few exotic sauces, which, although they have traditional uses, should be enjoyed on mundane foods, too. (Harissa on a hot dog is the bomb!) It is experiments like these that, to me, make cooking fun.

And then, there are some old standbys, which, when made with artisanal salts, seem new again. Best of all, these can, for the most part, be made in large batches that will last you a week or more—much more.

QUICK MANGO
CHUTNEY

TOMATO CHUTNEY

TAMARIND-DATE
CHUTNEY

TOMATO CHUTNEY

Makes 2 to 3 cups chutney

Fenugreek is critical in this recipe. A member of the legume family, this spice comes from the plant's seeds, and can be found both whole and ground. (I prefer spices whole whenever possible—they last longer, and have a better flavor when you toast and grind them yourself.) Fenugreek leaves are also used as a seasoning, both dried and fresh, and as salad greens. This recipe also calls for Kala Namak, the Indian black salt that you can read more about on page 19.

INGREDIENTS

1 tablespoon mustard oil (or neutral oil with ¼ teaspoon mustard seeds added)

1 tablespoon fenugreek seeds

5 to 6 fresh curry leaves (*kadi patta*) (see Glossary page 200), crushed, or 3 to 4 dried

3 garlic cloves

1 tablespoon peeled and grated fresh ginger

1 teaspoon mustard seeds

½ to 1 teaspoon crushed red pepper flakes (or more if you love heat)

¼ cup rice vinegar

3 large fresh and ripe tomatoes, chopped

1 teaspoon Kala Namak (Indian Black Salt), plus more to taste. *Although Kala Namak is the traditional salt, you can easily use another unrefined salt here. Try it with a Cyprus flake or a Japanese shio*

METHOD

1. Heat the mustard oil in a small sauté pan, add the fenugreek seeds and curry leaves and fry until fragrant, 1 to 2 minutes. Set aside to cool, then strain. (If you're using neutral oil, add the mustard seeds here, too.) Reserve the fragrant oil for salad dressings or sautéed fish.

2. Crush the garlic, ginger, mustard seeds, and red pepper flakes in a mortar with a pestle or in a coffee mill or small food processor. Add the fried fenugreek and curry leaves and continue to crush. Slowly add the vinegar to make a paste.

3. Add the paste back to the mustard oil in the pan and return to the heat. Add the tomatoes and the salt and bring to a simmer. Cook, stirring, for 30 minutes, or until the tomatoes break down. Cool and refrigerate the chutney. Remove the curry leaves and re-season with salt before serving cold alongside spicy dishes.

QUICK MANGO CHUTNEY

Makes 2 to 3 cups chutney

This recipe is based on the well-loved Major Grey's–style chutney. He was the nineteenth-century British Army officer who may or may not have invented it (or even existed). This chutney tastes best if it has some time to macerate, so make it a couple days ahead if you can. It also freezes well for up to a month, so make a double batch and use it for your next Indian feast.

INGREDIENTS

1 cup golden raisins

1 tablespoon vegetable oil

1 small red onion, diced

1 teaspoon crushed red pepper flakes

1 tablespoon peeled and grated fresh ginger

1 ripe mango, seeded and diced (or 2 cups frozen mango chunks, defrosted)

1 cup pineapple juice

¼ cup apple cider vinegar

¼ cup honey

½ cup chopped fresh cilantro leaves

1 teaspoon ground cumin (preferably freshly toasted and ground)

1 teaspoon Kala Namak (Indian Black Salt), plus more to taste. *Although Kala Namak is the traditional salt, you can easily use another unrefined salt here. Try it with a Hawaiian salt, Pangasinan Star, or something from any region where tropical fruit is abundant.*

METHOD

1. Cover the raisins with boiling water and set aside at room temperature to plump. (This can also be done with cold water overnight.)

2. Heat the oil in a large sauté pan over medium heat. Add the onion and red pepper flakes, and cook until the onion is translucent. Add the ginger and mango, and cook, stirring, until softened, about 2 minutes.

3. Slowly add the pineapple juice, vinegar, and honey and continue cooking at a simmer, stirring occasionally, for about 15 minutes, or until the mixture resembles a chunky jam.

4. Remove from the heat. Drian the plumped raisins, then stir them in with the cilantro, cumin, and salt. Set aside to cool completely. Store, refrigerated, or freeze for up to a month.

TAMARIND-DATE CHUTNEY

Makes 3 to 4 cups chutney

This chutney is a little saucier than the others, and it has the perfect balance of sweet and tang. This is thanks, in part, to the tamarind, a legume from the tamarind tree with a tart tangy pulp. You can find whole tamarind pods in well-stocked markets, or look for the paste, which is easier to use. This recipe also calls for jaggery, which is an unrefined raw cane and palm sugar commonly used throughout Asia and Africa (see Glossary page 201). It comes in bricks, much like Mexican piloncillo. You can easily substitute palm, date, or even brown sugar.

INGREDIENTS

1 teaspoon whole cumin seeds

1 teaspoon whole coriander seeds

¼ teaspoon crushed red pepper flakes

¾ cup tamarind paste, or 5 to 6 hulled and seeded pods

2 cups pitted dates

3 cups water

½ cup jaggery or brown sugar

1 teaspoon peeled and grated fresh ginger

1 teaspoon Kala Namak (Indian Black Salt), plus more to taste. *Although Kala Namak is the traditional salt, you can easily use another unrefined salt here. Try it with Himalayan, Bolivian, Mayan, or even a smoked salt.*

METHOD

1. Combine the cumin and coriander seeds in a dry sauté pan and heat until fragrant, about 1 minute. Cool, then pulverize, along with the red pepper flakes, in a coffee mill or in a mortar with a pestle. Set aside.

2. In a small saucepan, combine the tamarind, dates, and water and bring to a boil. Reduce to a simmer, and cook for 10 to 15 minutes until tender. Add the jaggery, ginger, reserved ground toasted spices, and salt. Simmer for another 10 minutes, then remove from the heat and cool.

3. Transfer the cooled chutney in a food processor and blend, adding water as needed, to achieve a thick puree. Pass the puree through a mesh strainer, then chill completely before serving. Serve with your favorite *chaat* (see Glossary page 200), or with anything savory and fried.

CHIMICHURRI

Makes 1 to 2 cups sauce

This sauce is probably Argentinean in origin, but it is popular throughout South America. It is terrific served over grilled beef or chicken, and also makes a wonderful marinade. There are a number of versions, as different as each region that loves it. There is no wrong recipe, and in fact, it works nicely with a variety of herbs. I like to use up the herbs that are on their last legs in my vegetable drawer. See the variations for some suggestions.

INGREDIENTS

½ teaspoon unrefined salt—*try Sal de Maras, Bolivian, Mayan, or a salt infused with herbs, roasted garlic, chiles, lime, capers, or peppercorns*

2 cups fresh flat-leaf parsley leaves

1 shallot or ¼ small red onion, roughly chopped

4 garlic cloves

½ teaspoon cumin seeds, toasted and ground

2 bay leaves, crumbled

½ teaspoon crushed red pepper flakes, or 1 fresh chile, such as a red jalapeño

¼ cup red wine vinegar, sherry wine vinegar and lemon juice, or champagne vinegar

½ cup olive oil

¼ teaspoon freshly ground black pepper

METHOD

1. Combine the salt, parsley, shallot, and garlic: pulverize in a food processor or in a mortar with a pestle.

2. Add the cumin seeds, bay leaves, red pepper flakes, vinegar, and finally the oil and process to a paste. Let macerate at room temperature for at least 30 minutes. Season with the black pepper, and more of the salt if needed.

VARIATIONS

—**Cilantro-churri.** Commonly seen in Paraguay and Uruguay, simply replace the parsley with fresh cilantro leaves.

—**Mixed Herbs.** Many recipes include a mix of herbs, including oregano, marjoram, cilantro, parsley, and even basil.

—**Rojo.** A common red version is made with either fresh tomatoes or canned tomato paste, paprika and/or chili powder, and sometimes roasted red peppers. Omit the fresh herbs, then add any or all of these red ingredients. Play around with it, then serve it with your best grilled beef.

HARISSA

Makes 1 to 2 cups harissa

This terrific North African condiment is one of my favorites. Used widely in the cuisines of Morocco, Algeria, and Tunisia (and every hipster enclave in America), the recipe varies, but generally contains olive oil, garlic, hot chiles, and spices. Use it as you would any hot condiment, or save it for your couscous and tagines. I am partial to harissa hot dogs.

INGREDIENTS

3 to 4 sun-dried tomatoes

1 to 2 dried red chiles, toasted and chopped—*try ancho, arbol, or New Mexican*

1 red bell pepper

½ teaspoon coriander seeds

½ teaspoon cumin seeds

½ teaspoon caraway seeds

1 teaspoon dried mint, or a handful of fresh mint leaves

1 teaspoon smoked paprika

3 garlic cloves

1 small red onion, minced

Finely grated zest and juice of 1 lemon

1½ tablespoons olive oil

½ teaspoon unrefined salt—*try Mali, Atlas Mountain, or a salt infused with cumin, coriander, chiles, mint, paprika, or olives*

METHOD

1. Cover the sun-dried tomatoes and red chiles with hot water and set aside to plump.

2. Roast the red pepper over an open flame (or under a broiler), turning, until the entire skin is charred black. Place in a bag or sealable container, close it tightly, and set it aside; the skin will loosen with the steam. When cool, rub off the charred skin, and remove the stems and seeds.

3. Meanwhile, toast the coriander, cumin, and caraway seeds in a dry skillet. Cool, then pulverize in a coffee mill or mortar with a pestle.

4. Drain the liquid from the sun-dried tomatoes and chiles and reserve it. Combine the tomatoes and chiles with the roasted red pepper and ground spices in a food processor or blender and pulverize. Add the mint, paprika, garlic, and onion and continue to process. Add the lemon zest, lemon juice, and oil. Adjust the consistency as needed with the reserved tomato and chile liquid. Add the salt last. Taste and adjust the seasoning as necessary. Store the harissa, airtight, in the refrigerator for 2 to 3 weeks, or freeze for longer storage.

VARIATIONS

—Green Harissa. Often thinner than red harissa, the green version is used more like a pesto, drizzled into soups or served as a dip. Use fresh serrano or jalapeño chiles in place of the dried red ones, omit the tomato and paprika, and replace it with 1 scallion, ½ cup fresh flat-leaf parsley, ½ cup fresh cilantro, and ½ cup fresh spinach leaves.

—Rosy Harissa. The most exotic versions of this sauce have a lovely floral essence. Add to the above recipe 1 large fresh tomato (perfectly ripe), a handful of rose petals, and ¼ cup rose water. Add 1 tablespoon of sugar and season with a little more lemon juice to taste.

MUSTARD

Makes about 1 cup mustard

A homemade mustard might sound pointless when there are so many mustards at the store already. But it is making foods like this from scratch that, to me, makes cooking exciting. Use the guidelines from this recipe and its variations to create something that is 100 percent you.

INGREDIENTS

¼ cup yellow mustard seeds

2 tablespoons brown mustard seeds

¼ cup white wine vinegar

¼ cup water

1 teaspoon fresh thyme leaves

1 teaspoon fresh tarragon leaves

1 to 2 teaspoons granulated sugar

½ teaspoon unrefined salt—*try Bavarian rock salt, especially if you plan to serve your mustard with sausages.*

METHOD

1. Combine the mustard seeds, vinegar, and water in a container with a tight-fitting lid. Set aside at room temperature for 2 to 3 days, until the liquid is absorbed and the seeds have softened.

2. Transfer the mustard seed mixture to a food processor. Add the thyme, tarragon, sugar, and salt and process until thick but still a little seedy. Store, airtight, in the refrigerator for several weeks.

VARIATIONS

—**Honey Mustard.** Omit the herbs, add 1 teaspoon prepared horseradish, and replace the sugar with ¼ cup honey.

—**Spicy Mustard.** Replace the thyme and tarragon with oregano and add 1 tablespoon canned chipotle chiles, Tabasco, or sriracha sauce during the blending.

KETCHUP

Makes about 1 quart ketchup

As my family will attest, I will eat just about anything. But one thing I cannot abide is prepared ketchup. Despite its ubiquity, it's pretty bad for you. Most are loaded with sugar (or corn syrup) and for me, the flavor is lackluster. I just don't want it anywhere near my fries. However, if I get the chance to make my own ketchup, then I am all in. It takes a little time, and the nonadventurous probably won't appreciate it. But if you like things that are interesting, then give it a try. You can use ground spices in this recipe, but it will be more flavorful if you use whole spices and grind them yourself.

INGREDIENTS

2 tablespoons olive oil

1 red onion, chopped

1 fennel bulb, chopped

1 celery stalk, chopped

1 teaspoon peeled and grated fresh ginger

2 garlic cloves, minced

1 teaspoon crushed red pepper flakes

1 teaspoon coriander seeds, toasted and ground

2 cloves, ground

3 to 4 allspice berries, ground

½ stick cinnamon, ground

¼ teaspoon crushed black peppercorns

½ teaspoon dry mustard powder

One 28-ounce can diced tomatoes with juices

1 tablespoon Worcestershire sauce

½ cup apple cider vinegar

¼ cup honey

1 teaspoon unrefined salt—*try an American sea salt, because ketchup.*

METHOD

1. Heat the oil in a large saucepan over medium-high heat. Add the onion, fennel, and celery and cook, stirring, until translucent. Add the ginger, garlic, red pepper flakes, coriander, cloves, allspice, cinnamon, peppercorns, and mustard powder. Cook for 3 to 5 minutes, stirring, until fragrant.

2. Add the tomatoes, Worcestershire, vinegar, honey, and salt. Reduce the heat and simmer, stirring occasionally, for 30 to 45 minutes until the sauce has thickened. Cool to room temperature.

3. Transfer to a blender and puree until smooth. Pass through a fine-mesh strainer, then chill it completely. Taste and adjust the seasoning if needed before serving. Store, airtight, in the refrigerator for up to a month.

VARIATIONS

—Srirachup. Add ¼ to ½ cup sriracha, replace the vinegar with ¼ cup of rice vinegar and ¼ cup lime zest and juice, add 1 cup of chopped fresh cilantro, and increase the honey to ½ cup.

—Fruity Ketchup. Add 2 cups of plumped dried fruit with the onions. Try raisins, currants, dried figs, dates, or a mixture. They will add both texture and sweetness—fantastic on salty fried foods.

KETCHUP

MUSTARD

GREMOLATA

Makes about 1 cup gremolata

This is the world's easiest condiment. Though traditionally an accompaniment to the Milanese classic *osso buco*, gremolata can brighten up many dishes. I keep a jar on hand in the fridge, and use it whenever my dinner seems a bit boring. Sprinkle it over seafood, pork, game, T-bones, grilled salads (see page 113), or bruschetta (see page 97). I even use it to liven up pizza and pasta.

INGREDIENTS

2 cups fresh flat-leaf parsley leaves

1 garlic clove

Finely grated zest of 1 lemon

½ teaspoon unrefined salt—*try any sel gris, fiore di sale, a smoked salt, or a salt infused with herbs, citrus, peppercorns, capers, anchovy, red wine vinegar, red wine, za'atar, or ash*

Pinch of freshly ground black pepper

METHOD

1. Combine the parsley leaves, garlic, and zest on a cutting board and mince together into a dry paste. Add the salt and pepper at the end of mincing. Store airtight in the fridge for several days, or freeze for longer storage.

VARIATIONS

—**Regional Differences.** There are some common versions of gremolata that include the addition of anchovies, grated pecorino Romano cheese, and toasted nuts. Ratios are left up to personal taste, but the general rule is that no one ingredient should overpower any of the others.

—**Persillade.** This is the French version, which contains no lemon zest—just parsley and garlic. It does, however, sometimes appear with olive oil or vinegar. I'd use a French salt here.

PASILLA AIOLI

Makes 2 to 3 cups aioli

Aioli, a.k.a. garlicky mayonnaise, should be in every cook's arsenal. It is the perfect accompaniment to so many things—fried foods, grilled meat and fish, not to mention fresh, roasted, grilled, steamed, or sautéed vegetables. This pasilla version has a slight chile kick, which I find a little more interesting. For the traditional version, you can simply leave out the chile paste. And you'll find even more variations following the recipe.

INGREDIENTS

1 whole head garlic

5 to 6 dried pasilla chile pods

1 large egg yolk

1 teaspoon fresh lemon juice

1 teaspoon water

½ teaspoon dry mustard powder

1½ cups canola oil

⅓ teaspoon freshly ground white pepper

½ teaspoon unrefined salt—*try Mayan, Manzanillo, smoked salt, or a salt infused with cumin, roasted garlic, or lime*

METHOD

1. Preheat the oven to 350°F. Wrap the garlic head in aluminum foil and roast until soft, about 45 minutes. Cool completely, then cut off the root end and squeeze out the soft garlic pulp. Set aside.

2. Meanwhile, toast the chile pods on a dry skillet, or in a hot oven, until fragrant and softened, 3 to 4 minutes. Allow to cool and crisp. Devein and deseed the pods, then place them in a saucepan and cover them with water. Bring to a boil, turn off the heat, and let steep for 30 to 60 minutes, or until the chile pods have softened.

3. Drain the chiles and reserve the liquid. Puree the pods in a blender until smooth, adding some of the liquid as necessary to facilitate the puree. Strain the chile paste and set aside. (Store leftover chile paste in the fridge for a week, or freeze it for long-term storage.)

4. In a large bowl, combine the egg yolk, lemon juice, water, and mustard powder. Whisk together, then slowly drizzle in half of the oil, whisking constantly. Done properly, it should take several minutes. It helps to anchor the bowl on a wet towel, draped inside a sauce-pan—double boiler–style, to keep it from spinning while you drizzle and whisk. When half the oil has been added, add the garlic, ¼ cup of chile paste, the white pepper, and salt. Continue whisking in the remaining oil. The mixture should emulsify into a thick, mayon-naise texture. When all the oil has been added, taste and adjust the seasoning with more salt, lemon juice, and more chile paste as needed. Use right away, or refrigerate for up to a week.

VARIATIONS

—**Sun-Dried Tomato.** Replace the chile paste with ¼ cup of reconstituted and pureed sun-dried tomatoes

—**Roasted Red Pepper.** Replace the chile paste with ¼ cup of pureed roasted red pepper.

—**Pesto.** Omit the mustard and replace the chile paste with ¼ cup of pesto.

—**Blender Aioli.** You can combine the chile, garlic, egg, lemon juice, and water in a blender then add the oil with the blender running. The advantage is speed and ease. The disadvantage is less control over the finished texture (it tends to get too thick). There is also some loss of finished product as it gets stuck in the blender blades and is hard to clean out. Food processors will work, too, although less successfully, because they spin the puree toward the outside of the bowl, which doesn't facilitate emulsification. If you triple or quadruple the recipe, however, the processor works just fine.

—**Trouble-shooting.** If your aioli is not thick, it is probably because the oil was not added slowly enough while whisking. (Or you mismeasured.) You can try again by substituting the "bad" aioli for the oil. Whisk it into another egg yolk—this time very slowly.

CHIMICHURRI

HARISSA

GREMOLATA

RAITA

Makes 3 to 4 cups raita

This Indian/Pakistani condiment is a cooling addition to a traditional spicy meal. But I like it with any spicy cuisine. It works surprisingly well with hot Mexican food, four-alarm chili, or your best hot barbecue. There are many versions from all over India, Pakistan, and Bangladesh. See the variations for some other examples.

INGREDIENTS

1 red onion, finely chopped

4 Persian cucumbers (or 1 English), scrubbed and grated

½ cup fresh cilantro leaves, chopped

1 teaspoon cumin seeds, toasted and ground

1½ cups plain yogurt

½ teaspoon Kala Namak (Indian Black Salt), plus more to taste—*although Kala Namak is the traditional salt, you can easily use another unrefined salt here. Try it with Maldon or Cyprus flake.*

METHOD

1. Put the chopped onion in a small bowl, cover with cold water, and let soak for 15 to 20 minutes, then drain. This leaches out the harsh oils that cause bad breath.

2. In a large bowl, combine cucumber, cilantro, drained onion, and cumin and toss together. Stir in the yogurt and black salt and set aside to macerate for 15 to 30 minutes.

3. Taste and re-season just before serving. Raita does not keep well, so make only as much as you need for one meal at a time.

VARIATIONS

—**Fruit Raita.** Replace the onion and cucumber with seasonal fruit. I like a mixture, keeping it either all sweet, like banana and apple, or all tart, like citrus and pineapple.

—**Vegetable Raita.** In addition to the cucumber, add grated carrot, chopped bell pepper, tomato, grated broccoli stem, or any other vegetable you have on hand.

—**Spinach Raita.** Replace the cucumber with 2 cups of spinach leaves, and add ½ teaspoon each of ground cardamom and ground ginger.

MEAT AND SEAFOOD

In my opinion, the best way to enjoy great salt is on a piece of great meat. Grilled rare, or sautéed briefly in a dab of butter, a simple piece of protein is the best thing to enhance, and be enhanced by, a wonderful salt. But one hardly needs a recipe for that. And frankly, even superb meat is boring when served plainly day after day. With that in mind, I offer you the following compilation of meat and seafood dishes. They will highlight your salts in marvelous ways.

I'm a meat lover, no doubt. But I also love animals. That dichotomy has led me to limit my meat consumption to 2 to 3 days a week, and to choose meat only from well-raised animals. It's not always easy, but the effort is good for my soul. The thing is, there are few foods that benefit more from a good salt. Protein needs a good salt if it's going to please my palate. If the meat isn't happy, and there is no good salt, I'll just have the salad then, thanks.

KAHLÚA PIG

Makes 6 to 8 servings

Kahlúa means to cook in an underground oven, and it is used, most often, to describe the traditional Hawaiian technique of cooking a whole pig in an imu, or pit. Layered with wood charcoal, hot stones, and banana leaves, this slow-cooking method results in tender, melt-in-your-mouth meat with a rich, smoky flavor. The use of alaea salt is also traditional, which means you can easily simulate this technique in your home oven or slow cooker. Aloha.

INGREDIENTS

One 5-pound boneless pork butt or shoulder roast

3 tablespoons Hawaiian alaea salt (use about ¾ teaspoon per pound of meat)

4 slices thick smoked bacon

3 banana leaves (available frozen in specialty markets; these are not essential, but are superfun)

Kitchen twine

METHOD

1. Preheat the oven to 300°F. Make several small slits around the surface of the roast, then rub it all over with the alaea. Wrap the roast in the bacon strips, then in banana leaves, and secure with twine. (If you're not using banana leaves, place the roast on a rack and drape the bacon over the top.)

2. Place the meat in a roasting pan fitted with a rack and fill the bottom of the pan with about an inch of water (until it just comes to the level of the rack). Cover tightly with aluminum foil or a lid and roast for 5 hours or until very tender. The meat should fall apart easily. Check periodically, and add more water to the pan if it has evaporated.

3. Rest the finished roast for 10 minutes, then carefully unwrap and shred. Sprinkle with the remaining salt before serving with roasted sweet potatoes, coleslaw, or poi (see Glossary page 202).

EASY SMOKED SAUSAGE

Makes about 4 large sausages

Homemade sausage is great on a number of levels—you can control the quality of meat and the type of seasoning; you also get a tremendous sense of accomplishment. This recipe is particularly miraculous, as it requires no special equipment (my favorite kind of recipe). The smoke in this version comes from smoked salt (either store-bought or homemade). If you are not a smoke fan, see the variations for other easy sausages.

INGREDIENTS

2 to 3 pounds ground beef (75 to 80% lean)

¾ cup very cold water

4 garlic cloves, minced

2 tablespoons mustard seeds, toasted and ground

3 tablespoons freshly ground black pepper

¼ to ½ teaspoon crushed red pepper flakes

2 tablespoons unrefined smoked salt

1 tablespoon Prague Powder #1

METHOD

1. In a large bowl, or the bowl of an electric stand mixer fitted with the paddle attachment, beat together the meat and water until well emulsified. Add the garlic, mustard seeds, black pepper, red pepper flakes, smoked salt, and Prague Powder and mix thoroughly.

2. Roll the meat into 2 to 3 sausage-shaped logs about 2 inches in diameter. Wrap them tightly in plastic wrap and chill for 24 hours.

3. The next day, preheat the oven to 350°F. Line a roasting pan with a rack to elevate the meat above the drippings. Unwrap the sausage, set them on the rack, and bake for 1 hour, or until the internal temperature registers 160°F. Serve immediately as a warm sausage, or cool, rewrap, and chill completely in the refrigerator for cold sliced sausage.

VARIATIONS

—Game Meat. This same recipe can be made with any ground meat you have on hand. It is particularly nice with venison. Be sure to check the internal temperature recommended for the type of meat you chose.

—Andouille. Spicy Louisiana-style sausage can be approximated by using ground pork (either all or part) and by adding to the existing spices an additional teaspoon each of freshly ground toasted cumin, paprika, dried thyme, dried oregano, and a pinch each of ground cloves and allspice. Cook this to 160°F as well.

CITRUS SHRIMP BROCHETTE

Makes 2 to 4 servings

Shrimp skewers are an easy crowd-pleaser, but they do take some preparation. This recipe is great because much of it can be done ahead of time. The bright, fresh flavors are perfect for summer barbecues, or when you feel like re-enacting summer.

INGREDIENTS

1 pound large shrimp (21/25), shelled and de-veined

4 garlic cloves, minced

¼ cup fresh flat-leaf parsley leaves, chopped

¼ cup chopped cilantro leaves

Finely grated zest and juice of 1 lemon

Finely grated zest and juice of 1 lime

Finely grated zest and juice of 1 orange

½ cup olive oil

Pinch of crushed red pepper flakes (optional)

1 teaspoon unrefined salt—try a Japanese shio, Manzanillo, Pangasinan Star, an American salt from the Gulf Coast, a smoked salt, or a salt infused with citrus, agave, vanilla, cumin, fennel, curry, seaweed, or sriracha.

METHOD

1. If using wooden skewers, soak them in cold water for at least 60 minutes. Overnight is even better.

2. In a large bowl, combine the shrimp, garlic, herbs, citrus zest (reserve the juices), olive oil, red pepper flakes (if desired), and ½ teaspoon of the salt. Toss to coat shrimp, then refrigerate and let marinate for at least 60 minutes. Overnight is better here, too.

3. Remove the shrimp from the marinade. Lay them on a cutting board in groups of 4 to 6, all facing the same direction. Thread two skewers through them at an equal distance from the center. This keeps the shrimp from spinning on the grill as they are flipped and promotes even cooking. Place in a pan and drizzle with the reserved citrus juices.

4. Preheat the grill on high (or use your broiler). Cook the skewers over medium-high heat for 3 to 5 minutes per side, until they turn pink. To serve, remove the skewer and sprinkle with the remaining salt. Serve with a simple salad, such as Butter Lettuce and Radish Slaw (page 113) or Grilled Greens Salad (page 113).

VARIATIONS

—**Curry Favor.** Add 2 tablespoons of your favorite curry paste or powder to the marinade. Then finish with Kamal Namak and serve over rice and tomato, mango, or Tamarind-Date Chutney (page 126).

—**Coconut.** Add ½ can of coconut milk to the marinade, use Hawaiian alaea salt, and serve with a sprinkle of toasted coconut.

—**Scallops.** Try the same technique with scallops.

BROILED LOBSTER TAIL WITH FENNEL

Makes 2 servings

Lobster is commonly considered a luxury food, but it wasn't always so. History records that lobsters along the Atlantic Coast were so plentiful that they were routinely used as bait for more desirable fish. But today, lobster signifies a celebration. While working as a culinary instructor for the US Navy, I learned that lobster is traditionally served to the crew on their last night underway. This could mean prepping anywhere from a couple of hundred lobsters on a small cargo ship to 7,000 of the crustaceans on a carrier. Needless to say, the CSs get pretty good at removing the shells. This recipe uses the sweetness of fennel to accentuate the sweetness of the shellfish—then complements them both with a bang of perfect salt.

INGREDIENTS

1 lobster tail

1 tablespoon olive oil

2 tablespoons unsalted butter

1 fennel bulb, halved and sliced (fronds reserved)

4 large shallots, sliced

½ cup white wine

Finely grated zest and juice of 1 lemon

Finely grated zest and juice of 1 orange

1 teaspoon unrefined salt—*try an American salt from the Northeast, a flor de sal, a Japanese shio, or a salt infused with vanilla, fennel, or citrus*

½ cup fresh chopped tarragon leaves

Crusty French bread, for serving

METHOD

1. Preheat the broiler. Cut down the length of the top of the lobster shell with kitchen shears. Drizzle it lightly with the olive oil, place on a baking sheet, and broil it for 5 to 10 minutes until the meat is opaque and the shells are browned. Cool until they can be handled, then remove the tail meat. Cut the meat into bite-size chunks and set aside.

2. Melt the butter in a large sauté pan. Add the fennel and shallots and cook, stirring, over medium heat, until tender and golden brown. Add the wine, lemon and orange zests, and lemon and orange juice, and ½ teaspoon of the salt. Continue cooking until the liquids have reduced by half.

3. Just before serving, add the lobster meat and tarragon and cook, stirring, for another minute to warm through. Finish with some of the reserved chopped fennel fronds and the remaining salt. Serve immediately with crusty French bread.

VARIATIONS

—Lobster Salad. For a chilled version of this dish (or the leftovers—if any remain) make a refreshing luncheon salad. Stir in some mayonnaise and a grated apple, then serve on a bed of arugula, watercress, or between two slices of great pumpernickel bread.

—Grilled. You can translate the cooking of the lobster and fennel to the grill for a charred, smoky version. Make the pan sauce separately, then finished with a smoked salt.

OYSTERS GRATIN

Makes 3 to 4 servings

This dish makes a stunning presentation when served in the individual oyster shells, nestled together in a superchunky rock salt. But oyster shucking is definitely an acquired skill. If you don't possess it, you can omit the shells (by buying preshucked oysters) and bake the whole thing in a shallow gratin dish. Mischief managed.

INGREDIENTS

2 to 3 cups very coarse but inexpensive rock salt (my local Asian market has several to choose from)

1 dozen shucked oysters (if canned, then well rinsed and drained)

1 teaspoon unrefined salt—*try Sogum, bamboo, fleur de sel, something from the Pacific Northwest, smoked, or a salt infused with capers, anchovy, lemon, fennel, red wine vinegar, or seaweed*

2 tablespoons unsalted butter

2 scallions, chopped

2 tablespoons whole wheat flour

1 cup half-and-half

¼ cup Gruyère cheese

Finely grated zest and juice of 1 lemon

¼ teaspoon freshly ground black pepper

METHOD

1. Preheat the broiler on high, or an oven to 500°F. Line an ovenproof dish with rock salt. Nestle the shucked oysters into the rock salt, about ½ inch apart. Sprinkle lightly with salt and refrigerate.

2. Melt the butter in a sauté pan over medium-high heat. Add the scallions and cook until translucent. Add flour and cook, stirring, until the flour has absorbed all the fat. (This is called a roux; see Glossary page 201.) Slowly drizzle in the half-and-half, stirring constantly, until all the liquid is in and the sauce is smooth. Remove from the heat, add the cheese, lemon zest and juice, and the pepper. (This is a modified Mornay sauce.)

3. Place a generous dollop of sauce on top of each oyster. Place the dish on a baking sheet and place it under the broiler. Broil until golden brown and bubbly, 2 to 4 minutes. Rotate if necessary for even coloration.

4. Place the hot gratin dishes on a napkin-lined plate and serve immediately with another pinch of the salt.

OYSTERS WITH
MIGNONETTE SAUCE

OYSTERS GRATIN

OYSTERS WITH MIGNONETTE SAUCE

Makes 2 to 4 servings

This is my personal favorite way to eat oysters. The name comes from the OG method of peppercorn crushing. It is done with brute strength, pressing down on the spice with the bottom of a sauté pan. Forget cocktail sauce. This simple, spicy, acidic concoction is, for me, the perfect counterpoint to briny shellfish. I like to make my sauce a few hours ahead, to give the flavors a chance to marry.

INGREDIENTS

1 teaspoon black peppercorns

½ teaspoon pink peppercorns

1 teaspoon unrefined salt—*try Japanese shio, bamboo, flor de sal, something from the American Pacific Northwest or Northeast, a smoked salt, or a salt infused with peppercorns, citrus, herbs, fennel, shallots, or red wine*

1 shallot, minced

1 cup good-quality red wine vinegar

1 dozen fresh oysters (or more—more is better), shucked, on the half shell

METHOD

1. Place the peppercorns (black and pink) on a cutting board. Hold a small sauté pan firmly, with one hand on the handle and the other on the rim. Press down in a rolling motion over peppercorns, crushing them all roughly. Repeat a few times, until all the peppercorns are cracked.

2. Combine the peppercorns, salt, shallot, and vinegar in a small saucepan and bring to a simmer. Turn off heat and set aside to steep and macerate for at least 1 hour, or overnight.

3. Shuck the oysters, being careful to keep all the liquid (a.k.a. oyster liquor) in the bottom half of the shell. Nestle the shucked oysters into an oyster dish or a plate of crushed ice. Present the shucked oysters with a ramekin of the mignonette sauce and a small spoon. Eat the oysters with a generous spoonful of mignonette sauce on top of each one.

TUNA POKE

Makes 4 to 6 servings

The word *poke* in Hawaiian means "to slice," and this is a traditional dish of fish (most commonly yellowfin tuna) that is sliced into bite-size pieces and seasoned. Traditional ingredients include sea salt and *inamona*, a kukui nut paste (see Glossary page 201) made from the same nuts that are painted and strung into leis. The macadamia nut, which has a similar texture, can be used instead, although its taste is less bitter. You can pick up some inamona paste at the Maui Whole Foods if you are lucky like that.

INGREDIENTS

2 pounds best-quality, freshest tuna available (sashimi grade)

1 teaspoon alaea salt

¼ cup soy sauce

1 scallion, finely chopped

½ large yellow Maui onion, thinly sliced

1 tablespoon sesame oil

1 tablespoon peeled and grated fresh ginger (optional)

1 fresh red chile pepper, minced, or 1 teaspoon crushed red pepper flakes (optional)

1 tablespoon toasted sesame seeds

1 tablespoons *inamona* (see Glossary page 201), or ground, toasted, salted macadamias

METHOD

1. Cut the tuna into long fillets, about 1 inch thick, then slice into cubes. Pat dry to remove any moisture. Salt with the alaea and set aside in the fridge.

2. In a large bowl, combine soy sauce, scallion, yellow onion, sesame oil, and optional ginger and chile. Whisk together, then add the tuna and toss well to coat. Cover and refrigerate for 1 hour.

3. Serve the poke garnished with sesame seeds and inamona. Eat it with lettuce leaves for pinching, or over a bowl of short-grain Japanese sushi rice, seasoned with rice vinegar and kombu.

VARIATIONS

—**Mayonnaise Poke.** A thick version of poke is made with the addition of spicy mayonnaise, which is nothing more than regular mayo mixed with your favorite chile sauce.

—**California Poke.** The addition of a diced avocado is never wrong (although it is not Hawaiian). Cherry tomatoes and diced cucumber are equally outrageous on the Islands, but welcome on the tongue.

FORBIDDEN
RICE SALAD

PAN-FRIED MACKEREL WITH GRAPEFRUIT MINT PESTO

Makes 2 servings

Mackerel is a fish mostly appreciated by other, larger fish. And although it has been historically popular, it is no longer a common American menu item. It is traditionally known as a stinky fish, because it spoils fast. But modern refrigeration makes good mackerel readily available. Recognize it by its striped back and V-shaped tail. It is deliciously rich and benefits from spicy, acidic accompaniments.

INGREDIENTS

1 large grapefruit (ruby red if available)

½ large purple onion, minced

1 cup fresh mint leaves, minced

1 cup fresh tarragon or basil leaves, minced

1 teaspoon unrefined salt—*try Mali, Manzanillo, something Hawaiian, smoked, or a salt infused with citrus, mint, fennel, red wine vinegar, wasabi, saffron, sriracha, or Szechuan peppercorns*

1 teaspoon Dijon mustard

2 tablespoons olive oil

2 whole mackerel, cleaned and gutted (keep the skin on, and the head if you wish)

½ teaspoon freshly ground black pepper

2 tablespoons unsalted butter

METHOD

1. Finely grate the zest of the grapefruit, and combine it on a cutting board with the onion, mint, tarragon, and ½ teaspoon of the salt. Chop them together to create a dry paste, then set aside in a large bowl.

2. Slice the now-bald rind and pith off the grapefruit, and cut out the meaty segments between the membrane (these are known as *suprêmes*). Add the grapefruit suprêmes to the bowl, along with the mustard and 1 tablespoon of the olive oil. Mix well and set aside at room temperature.

3. Season the filets with the remaining salt and pepper. Heat a cast-iron (or very heavy) skillet over high heat. Add the remaining 1 tablespoon oil and the butter. As soon as the fat is hot, add the fish and cook until golden brown, 3 to 4 minutes. Carefully flip the fish and cook for another 3 to 4 minutes, or to the desired doneness. Remove the fish from the pan and keep warm.

4. Add the grapefruit pesto to the empty fish pan and cook, stirring, for another minute to warm through. Serve each fillet topped with a generous portion of grapefruit mint pesto sauce.

VARIATIONS

—Rhubarb. Cook the fillets as directed, but instead of the grapefruit pesto, serve the fish on top of a bed of arugula or other sharp flavored green, dressed with chopped rhubarb pickles (see page 67).

—Chutney or Vinaigrette. Any tangy or acidic accompaniment works wonders with mackerel. Try Tomato Chutney (page 125), Mango Chutney (page 125), or Harissa (page 130).

SALT CRUST FISH

Makes 4 to 6 servings

This recipe has ancient roots in Silk Road extravagance. Probably originating in the Mediterranean salt-producing areas, it spread as far as China. You can salt-crust anything, (chicken was an early Chinese variation), but I like fish the best. Typically seen in magazines with salmon, I use it on whatever fish looks fresh at the market.

INGREDIENTS

One 3-pound whole fish (or the equivalent), such as sea bass, trout, snapper, bream, or salmon, cleaned and scaled

1 lemon, sliced into rounds

1 large bunch fresh thyme

2 large egg whites

5 cups unrefined sea salt—use something that is not too expensive, as you'll need a lot. I usually pick up a big bag of coarse Korean sea salt from my local Asian market (99 Ranch!)

Good-quality olive oil, for serving

Lemon wedges, for serving

METHOD

1. Preheat the oven to 450°F. Rinse the fish and pat dry with paper towels. Open the cavity, fill it with the lemon slices and thyme sprigs, then close it back up and set the fish aside.

2. In a large bowl, whip the egg whites to a light froth (no peaks necessary—just break up the albumen) then fold in the salt. The mixture should resemble wet sand. The result may vary with the salt type, so add a little water or more salt as necessary.

3. Pat out the salt in the center of an ovenproof serving platter. Make your salt pile slightly larger than your fish, and about ½-inch thick. Place the prepared fish on top, then pack the rest of the salt around and on top, completely sealing in the fish. (Some chefs like to leave the head and tail exposed, but I think it comes out better when completely sealed. You can always sculpt your salt into a fish face.) Place the pan into the preheated oven and bake for 25 to 30 minutes. (The internal temperature for fish varies, and is subject to preference. But in general, aim for around 130°F.)

4. Remove the fish from the oven and cool slightly, then present it at the table, where you can crack open the salt crust with the wack of a spoon. It comes off easily in big chunks, exposing a perfectly cooked whole fish, which can then be divided up among your guests. Serve with a simple accompaniment of good olive oil and lemon wedges.

VARIATIONS

—**Citrus Fish.** Orange, grapefruit, and lime make a nice filling, separately or together. For a real citrus punch, layer the outside of the fish with citrus slices as well, before you build the salt crust.

—**Herbs.** Thyme is certainly not your only option. Try fresh lavender, cilantro, sage, mint, really anything goes. And consider adding a spice blend or flavorful condiment to the cavity. Try curries, Harissa (page 130), pesto, or a ready-made spice blend like za'atar or furikake (see Glossary pages 203 and 201).

SALT BLOCK SEARING AND GRILLING

Makes 2 to 4 servings

The coolest thing about Himalayan salt blocks is their ability to retain heat. They are not something I would routinely cook on, but there is no denying that tableside searing is a showstopper. The method works best with thin, quick-cooking seafood or thinly sliced, high-quality beef. The basic method is explained below, with endless options to shift your creativity into gear.

INGREDIENTS

1 large block Himalayan salt

¼ cup olive oil

1 pound meat, poultry, or seafood (such as scallops, shrimp, calamari, octopus, tuna, or salmon), washed, trimmed, and sliced if necessary into no thicker than 1-inch bite-size pieces

1 to 1½ cups of an accompanying sauce, such as a pesto, salsa, aioli, harissa, gremolata, etc. (see the section Sauces, Condiments, and Dressings)

FOR SEARING

Place the dry salt block on a baking sheet and place in a cool oven. Turn the heat to 400°F and gradually heat the salt block. When the oven has reached temperature, keep heating the block for another 30 minutes. Place the hot block on a heatproof platter and bring it to the table with the prepared meat or seafood. Sear the meat on the hot salt block for 2 to 3 minutes. Flip it with tongs and cook another 2 to 3 minutes. Serve immediately with the selected sauce. Let the block cool down completely to room temperature for several hours, then scrub it with cold water.

FOR GRILLING

Place the dry salt block on a cool barbecue grill. Light the flame and let it heat gradually to 400°F, then continue heating it there for another 30 minutes. Working on the grill, place the prepared meat or seafood onto the hot salt block and sear for 2 to 3 minutes. Flip it with tongs, and cook another 2 to 3 minutes. Serve immediately with the selected sauce. Let the block cool down completely to room temperature for several hours, then scrub it with cold water.

VARIATIONS

—**Marinated.** You can use a marinated meat instead of (or in addition to) an accompanying sauce.

—**Vegetables.** Meat is not the only thing that sears. Try slices of zucchini, eggplant, winter squash, and mushrooms. You can even sear marinated tofu.

BAKING

I am the rare chef who is also a baker. I was trained to do it all, and I firmly believe that a good chef must have a handle on all aspects of the kitchen. Along with that comes the ability to make a great meal from start to finish. But, as a culinary instructor, I've learned that not everyone is as comfortable in the bakery as they are in other parts of a kitchen—even though baking is no different from the rest of cooking. The same reactions occur in an oven as they do on a grill, just in different forms. Proteins solidify, fats melt, gas expands—and good salt is just as crucial. Not just because salt brings out the delicious nuances in the flavor of simple grain. It is also crucial to fermentation, keeping yeast in check, and helping to develop the very structure of a crumb. So give baking a chance. If you screw it up, all you've lost is a little time and a little money. But you'll gain knowledge and you'll learn from your mistakes. Lecture over.

WHOLE GRAIN
CRACKERS

WATER
CRACKERS

SMOKE SALT
CHEESE LINED
WITH ASH

HERBED CHEESE
LINED WITH FIG
LEAVES

LEMON PEPPER
CHEESE

BUTTER CRACKERS

AN ASSORTMENT OF CRACKERS

When you take the time to make your own cheese, cure your own meats, and preserve your own pickles, you may as well make your own crackers. They are crazy easy, and crazy impressive. And there are few foods that highlight fancy salt better. Here are a few cracker possibilities. You can make the dough ahead of time, and you can make the crackers ahead of time, too. Freeze them in airtight containers until you need them.

WATER CRACKERS

Makes about 2 dozen crackers

INGREDIENTS

½ cup all-purpose flour

½ teaspoon unrefined salt—*try sel gris, fleur de sel, or a finely ground Bavarian, Himalayan, or Bolivian rock salt*

1 tablespoon unsalted butter

2 tablespoons very cold water

Finishing salt—*finish with the same salt, or add something unique, such as a smoked salt, a charcoal-infused black salt, or a salt infused with sesame, nuts, fennel, seaweed, or tea*

METHOD

1. In a medium bowl, combine the flour and salt. Cut in the butter with fingertips or a pastry cutter until the mixture resembles a coarse meal. Add the water and stir to create a firm dough. Wrap in plastic and rest the dough for 30 minutes in the refrigerator. (You can store this in the fridge overnight, or freeze it for up to a month.)

2. Turn the dough out onto a floured surface and, using a rolling pin, roll the dough out paper thin, ⅓- to ¼-inch thick. (You can also roll smaller portions of this dough out using a pasta machine for uniform thickness.) Pierce the dough all over with the tines of a fork (this is called docking), then place on a dry baking sheet and chill for 10 minutes.

3. Preheat the oven to 375°F. Coat a baking sheet with nonstick cooking spray. Return chilled, rolled, docked dough to the floured work surface and sprinkle with finishing salt. Cut into the desired shape, using a pastry wheel, cookie cutters, or a knife. Work quickly to maintain the crackers' shape. (The warmer the dough, the more they lose their shape when handled.)

4. Place the crackers on the prepared baking sheet. They can sit close together, as they will not expand in the oven. Bake until the edges are brown, 10 to 15 minutes, rotating the baking sheet occasionally to ensure even coloration. Cool completely and serve or store airtight at room temperature for a few days. Freeze for longer storage.

BUTTER CRACKERS

Makes about 2 dozen crackers

INGREDIENTS

1 cup whole-wheat flour

1 cup all-purpose flour

3 teaspoons baking powder

1 tablespoon granulated sugar

½ teaspoon unrefined salt—*try an American sea salt from the Northeast, any sel gris, or a finely ground Jurassic rock salt*

6 tablespoons (¾ stick/3 ounces) unsalted butter, chilled and diced

1 tablespoon vegetable oil

⅔ cup very cold water

1 egg yolk

1 tablespoon whole milk

2 tablespoons unsalted butter, melted

½ teaspoon finishing salt—*finish with the same salt, or add something unique, such as a smoked salt, a charcoal-infused black salt, or a salt infused with herbs, citrus, roasted garlic, maple, olives, bacon, or red wine*

METHOD

1. In a large bowl, combine the flours, baking powder, sugar, and the salt. Cut in chilled butter until the mixture resembles a coarse meal. Stir in the oil and water to create a firm dough. Wrap in plastic and chill in the fridge for at least 30 minutes. (You can store this in the fridge overnight, or freeze it for up to a month.)

2. Turn the dough out onto a floured surface and, using a rolling pin, roll the dough out to a ¼-inch thickness. (You can also roll smaller portions of this dough out using a pasta machine for uniform thickness.)

3. Mix together the egg yolk and milk to create an egg wash, then brush it over the surface of the dough. Pierce the dough all over with the tines of a fork (this is called docking), then place on a dry baking sheet and chill in the fridge for 10 minutes.

4. Preheat the oven to 400°F. Coat a baking sheet with nonstick cooking spray. Return the chilled, rolled, docked dough to the floured work surface. Cut into the desired shape, using a pastry wheel, cookie cutters, or knife. (I like to use a 1- to 2-inch scalloped circle cutter for these—so it looks kind of ritzy.) Work quickly to help maintain the crackers' shape. (The warmer the dough, the more they will lose their shape when handled.) Place the cut crackers on the prepared baking sheet and bake until golden brown, 8 to 10 minutes.

5. While the crackers bake, mix together melted butter with the finishing salt. As soon as you remove the crackers from the oven, brush the butter mixture on each hot cracker.

WHOLE GRAIN CRACKERS

Makes about 2 dozen crackers

INGREDIENTS

½ cup steel cut oats

1⅔ cup water

⅓ cup olive oil

½ teaspoon unrefined salt—*try flor de sal, an American salt from the Pacific Northwest, or a charcoal-infused black salt*

1 teaspoon baking powder

1 teaspoon flaxseeds

1 teaspoon sesame seeds

1 teaspoon chia seeds

1 teaspoon poppy seeds

2 to 3 cups whole-wheat flour

1 egg white, beaten

Finishing salt—*finish with the same salt, or add something unique, such as a smoked salt, a charcoal-infused black salt, or a salt infused with onion, thyme, lemon, sesame, peppercorns, seaweed, or kale*

METHOD

1. Combine the oats and water in a microwaveable container and heat in the microwave for 2 minutes. Set aside to soften. (Alternatively, bring the oats and water to a boil in a saucepan on the stovetop, then turn off the heat and let it sit.)

2. In a large bowl, combine the water, oil, and ½ teaspoon of the salt. Using a fork, stir in baking powder, flaxseeds, sesame seeds, chia seeds, poppy seeds, and cooled oats. Slowly add enough whole-wheat flour to create a firm dough. Turn the dough out onto a floured surface and knead for 5 minutes, adding more flour only to reduce stickiness. Return the dough to the bowl, cover, and rest at room temperature for 15 minutes. (You can store this in the fridge overnight, or freeze it for up to a month.)

3. Preheat the oven to 400°F. Coat a baking sheet with nonstick cooking spray. Turn the dough out onto a floured surface and divide it into 3 equal portions. With a rolling pin, roll each portion out to a ¼-inch thickness. (You can also roll smaller portions of this dough out using a pasta machine for uniform thickness.) Pierce the dough all over with the tines of a fork. (This is called docking). Brush the surface lightly with egg white, then sprinkle evenly with the finishing salt. Place on a prepared baking sheet and bake until the edges are brown, 10 to 15 minutes, rotating the pan occasionally to ensure even coloration. Cool completely.

4. I like to serve these crackers in rustic, large broken shards. But if you are the daintier sort, feel free to cut them into shapes with a knife or cookie cutter before baking. Just be sure to chill the rolled, docked dough before you cut them, to prevent shrinkage.

FOCACCIA JARDINIÈRE

Make 4 individual focaccia

In the United States, focaccia has been bastardized into a trendy sandwich bread. But it was traditionally a regional flat bread, topped simply with salt, oil, and maybe one other local ingredient. The following recipe is my favorite version—a handful of peppery greens, roasted to a crisp, and liberally salted. That's not to say I won't accept a focaccia sandwich, if you're offering.

INGREDIENTS

1 cup warm water

1 tablespoon honey

1¾ teaspoons active dry yeast (1 package)

½ cup whole-wheat flour

1 cup olive oil

3 teaspoons unrefined salt—*try fiore di sale, Japanese shio, Piran, a smoked salt, or a salt infused with lemon, roasted garlic, shallot, anchovy, red wine, horseradish, chiles, or tarragon*

1½ to 2 cups bread flour

2 tablespoons cornmeal

4 cups arugula

Finely grated zest and juice of ½ lemon

METHOD

1. In a large bowl, stir together the water, honey, and yeast, and set aside until foamy, about 5 minutes. Using a fork, stir in the whole-wheat flour to create a loose batter. Cover and set aside in a warm spot until it begins to bubble, 45 to 60 minutes. This is the sponge.

2. Add to the sponge ½ cup of the olive oil, 1 teaspoon of the salt, and enough bread flour to create a firm dough. Turn the dough out onto a floured surface and knead, adding flour only as necessary to reduce stickiness. Knead for 8 to 10 minutes until the dough becomes smooth and elastic. Return to the bowl, cover with a warm damp towel, and set aside to rise until doubled in volume, about 1 hour.

3. Preheat the oven to 450°F. Coat two baking sheets lightly with olive oil or nonstick cooking spray, then sprinkle evenly with cornmeal. (This keeps it from sticking, but more importantly, gives the finished bread the illusion of having been cooked on an open hearth.) Turn the risen dough out onto floured surface, and divide into 4 equal portions. Flatten each dough into ½-inch-thick disks. This will take a few minutes, as the elastic dough will spring back a bit. Shape it, let it rest, then shape it again, until it is the size you want. Place the dough on the prepared baking sheets (2 per pan), brush the surface with olive oil, and sprinkle with salt. Cover with plastic wrap and set aside for 10 minutes to proof. Meanwhile, toss the arugula with a tablespoon of the olive oil, the lemon zest and juice, and a generous pinch of the salt.

4. When the dough feels slightly puffed, unwrap and top each with the dressed arugula salad. Bake until the dough is golden brown and the greens are singed, 10 to 20 minutes, rotating the pan as needed to promote even baking. Serve immediately with a final pinch of salt.

VARIATIONS

—**Plain and Simple.** This bread, without the salad, is just as heavenly. Try adding a fresh grating of your favorite hard cheese just as the bread comes out of the oven.

—**Sandwich**. It is easy to make this bread into a sandwich loaf. Press the entire recipe into a 9 x 13-inch brownie pan and bake as desired, minus the greens. When cool, cut in half horizontally with a good serrated knife.

METHOD

1. Stir together 1 cup of the water with the yeast and set aside until foamy, about 10 minutes. Add 1 cup of the bread flour, and stir to create a batter consistency. Cover with a warm damp towel and set aside at room temperature for at least 1 hour. This is the sponge. (You can do this step overnight for maximum flavor.)

2. Add to the sponge an additional 1 cup of the water, the sugar, oil, 2 teaspoons of the salt, and enough flour to create a soft dough. Turn the dough out onto a floured surface and knead for 8 to 10 minutes until smooth and elastic. Return to the bowl, dust with flour, and cover again with a warm damp towel. Set aside at room temperature until doubled in volume, about 1 hour.

3. Turn the risen dough out onto a floured work surface and shape into a rope about 3 inches thick. Cut 2-inch pieces off the rope, and roll each of them into a tight ball. Cover loosely with plastic wrap and rest for 10 minutes.

4. Preheat the oven to 425°F. Spray a baking sheet with nonstick cooking spray, and sprinkle evenly with cornmeal.

5. Mix the egg with a tablespoon of water to make an egg wash; set aside. Combine 2 quarts of water with the baking soda and the remaining 1 teaspoon salt in a large deep pot. Bring to a boil, then reduce to a simmer.

6. Working with one ball at a time, form into a thin rope, about a foot long. Twist into a pretzel shape by bringing the ends of the rope to the center, crossing or twisting, then attaching to the center of the rope by pressing firmly. Drop each formed pretzel into the simmering liquid and poach for 30 seconds on each side. Remove with a spider or slotted spoon, tap off excess liquid, and place on the prepared baking sheet with the prettiest side facing up. Brush lightly with the egg wash, sprinkle with finishing salt, and bake until golden brown, 15 to 20 minutes, rotating the pan as needed for even browning. Transfer to a rack and cool completely before serving with Mustard (page 131)—and beer.

VARIATION

—**Beer Sticks.** These straight pretzels are basically poached bread sticks. Roll thinner ropes and poach them as you do with the traditional pretzel shape. They swim around in the liquid like water snakes. Arrange them directly on a baking sheet coated with pan spray, or give them a little curve. Cook them a little crisper than you would a soft pretzel.

OPPOSITE: PRETZELS AND BEER STICKS

SCANDINAVIAN POTATO FLATBREAD (LEFSE)

Makes about 15 lefse

This is my family's favorite Christmas tradition. We smear it with butter and eat it with various other traditional dishes from our melting pot of ancestors. (Although, in all honesty, it is often consumed directly off the griddle, hunkered over the kitchen sink.) In the homeland it is frequently served as a sweet treat with sugar and jam—but not in our house. We are a savory bunch.

INGREDIENTS

2 pounds russet potatoes

water as needed

2 teaspoons unrefined salt—*try Læsøe, Saltverk, Maldon, Halen Môn, sel gris, Viking smoked salt, or a salt infused with herbs, fennel, caraway, or cardamom*

3 to 4 cups all-purpose flour

METHOD

1. Peel and halve the potatoes. Place in a large pot, cover with cold water, and bring to a boil. Reduce the heat and cook at a simmer until the potatoes are tender, about 30 minutes. Drain and cool. (I often do this step the night before.)

2. Pass the cooled potatoes through a ricer (or press through a wire mesh strainer), then combine in a large bowl with the salt. Stir in the flour, 1 cup at a time, until you create a firm dough. Turn the dough out onto a floured work surface and knead for 3 to 5 minutes until smooth. Add additional flour only to reduce stickiness. Cover the dough and rest it for 20 minutes.

3. Preheat a griddle on medium-high heat. Divide the dough into four pieces, then roll each into thick ropes. Cut off golf ball–size pieces and roll into balls. With floured fingers, pat the balls into thin disks. Then, using a rolling pin, roll into circles ¼-inch thick. Cook on the hot, dry griddle until lightly golden but still pliable, 1 to 2 minutes per side. Repeat with the remaining dough. Serve warm. To store, cool, wrap airtight, and keep for up to a week in the refrigerator. Freeze for longer storage.

SNOWSHOE NAAN

Makes about 8 naan

This traditional Indian flatbread is often flavored with peppery nigella seeds (a.k.a. black onion seeds), and cooked on the side of a scorching hot tandoori oven. Slapping the dough on the side of the tandoor gives it the snowshoe shape. At home I simulate this effect through the forming, and use my cast-iron griddle, or my barbecue grill. So far, no one has complained.

INGREDIENTS

1 cup warm water

1 tablespoon granulated sugar

1¾ teaspoons active dry yeast (1 package)

¼ cup plain yogurt

1 tablespoon nigella seeds (optional; see variations)

1 teaspoon unrefined salt—*try Kala Namak for a traditional flavor*

2 to 3 cups bread flour

2 to 4 tablespoons ghee or unsalted butter, melted

METHOD

1. In a large bowl, combine the water, sugar, and yeast and stir to dissolve. Let stand until foamy, about 5 minutes. Add the yogurt, nigella seeds, salt, and enough bread flour to create a firm dough. Turn the dough out onto a floured surface and knead for 8 to 10 minutes until smooth and elastic. Add more flour only to reduce stickiness. Cover the dough with a warm, damp towel and set aside to rise at room temperature until doubled in volume, about 1 hour.

2. Preheat a griddle or grill on high. Divide the dough into 8 equal portions and roll into balls. Pat the balls into flat disks, then elongate into ovals with your fingertips. You may need to rest the dough for 2 to 3 minutes while forming to relax the dough's elasticity.

3. Brush one side of the ovals with ghee, and place on the hot griddle, ghee side down. Cook 2 to 4 minutes, until golden brown on the bottom and puffy. Brush the uncooked side with more ghee, flip, and brown again. Sprinkle with a final pinch of salt and serve warm.

VARIATIONS

—Onion or Garlic. Add ½ cup of sautéed and cooled onion or garlic (or both) with the yogurt, and proceed as directed.

—Sesame. Replace the nigella seeds with toasted sesame seeds, and add ½ teaspoon of toasted sesame oil with the yogurt.

ABOUT KNEADING

Kneading is either the thing you love about bread making, or the thing you hate about it. I'm a lover, which is why my recipes always refer to hand kneading. I just don't think that home machines do a good enough job. It is a crucial step, creating an elastic protein structure that traps the gasses of fermentation. Good mechanical kneading requires a dough hook that is shaped like a corkscrew. But home stand mixers generally come with a dough hook that is shaped like a fish hook. The dough just grabs it and holds on, spinning, but not kneading. So, I opt for the old-fashioned method for a better outcome. But that's me, and you should feel free to knead as you see fit. The same time rules apply, whether kneading by hand or machine—generally 8 to 10 minutes.

SWEETS

DOUBLE CHOCOLATE FUDGE COOKIES
CLASSIC PEANUT BRITTLE
TOFFEE WITH WHITE CHOCOLATE AND MACADAMIA
SMOKED PENUCHE FUDGE
MILK CHOCOLATE-ANISE CARAMELS
SALTED HONEY-DATE CARAMELS
SALTED TRUFFLES
VANILLA PANNA COTTA
NO-CHURN SALTED CHOCOLATE ICE CREAM
JAL JEERA POPSICLES
NO-CHURN MELON MINT SORBET
SALTED CARAMEL SAUCE
KHARA LASSI GRANITA
CRISP, SALTY MERINGUES

No good dessert was ever made without salt. There. I said it. Salt is a crucial component that brings out flavor, and ties all flavors together. It is just as important in pastry as it is in grilling, and roasting, and sauces, and everything else. Maybe a little more important, because pastry has a tendency to be overly sweet—a trait easily tamed by good salt. And lest you think the salt in pastry is just a fad (popularized by salted caramel and chocolate-covered bacon) let me remind you that sweet and salt have been together forever—Prosciutto and Melon, Sweet-and-Sour Pork, Cracker Jacks, Corn Dogs—case closed.

These days I regularly feature salt as a central component in dessert. The first time I did that, however, was by accident. My youngest daughter's seventh birthday party was a glorious park affair, with games, a piñata, a hello kitty cake, and hand-churned ice cream made in an old-fashioned crank machine that I found at a garage sale. FYI—hand-cranking by kids must be monitored. It tipped over two to three times, and salt water from the melting ice found its way into the ice cream. The too-polite kids ate it anyway, with quizzical looks.

DOUBLE CHOCOLATE FUDGE COOKIES

Makes about 2 dozen cookies

I like to use ebony, or extra-dark, cocoa powder. It has long been available to chefs (it's the one they use in Oreo cookies), and happily it's now available to home cooks. I also like bittersweet chocolate chunks, but you can use any chunk you like: milk, white, butterscotch—even carob. (Although what's the point of that?) You can use any nut you want, too. Come to think of it, this recipe is really just a chocolaty suggestion.

INGREDIENTS

16 tablespoons (2 sticks/8 ounces) unsalted butter, softened

1 cup granulated sugar

1 cup packed dark brown sugar

1½ teaspoons unrefined salt—*try Bali Pyramid, Maldon, flor de sal, or a salt infused with chocolate, espresso, vanilla, saffron, chiles, or matcha*

2 large eggs

1 teaspoon pure vanilla extract

½ cup extra-dark cocoa powder

1 teaspoon baking powder

2¼ cups all-purpose flour

2 cups chopped bittersweet chocolate chunks

1 cup toasted pecan pieces

METHOD

1. Preheat the oven to 350°F. Coat a baking sheet with nonstick cooking spray and set aside.

2. In a large bowl, cream together the butter and white and brown sugars until smooth and lump-free. Add 1 teaspoon of the salt and the eggs, one at a time. Add the vanilla and stir to incorporate thoroughly. Stir in the cocoa, baking powder, and then the flour in 2 to 3 increments. Fold in chocolate and cooled nuts.

3. Using an ice cream scoop, or two spoons, drop walnut-size balls of dough onto the prepared baking sheet, spacing them 1 inch apart. Sprinkle the top with remaining ½ teaspoon salt, and bake for 12 to 18 minutes, until firm. Cool completely, and store airtight.

VARIATIONS

—**Regular Chocolate Chip.** If you guessed that this is just a modified chocolate chip cookie recipe, you're right. If you want to get back to the original, omit the cocoa powder and make up that difference with more flour. Then try finishing with Murray River, Black Lava, or Black Diamond salt.

—**Chocolate Medley.** Use whatever kind of chocolate chip you like. Or use your favorite candy or chopped-up candy bar. Or omit the extra chocolate altogether and use dried cherries—not that anyone will be happy about that switch. Ya gotta do what ya gotta do.

—**Mexican Chocolate.** To simulate the flavors of Mexican hot chocolate in a cookie, add ½ teaspoon of ground cinnamon, ¼ teaspoon of cayenne or other hot chile powder, use chopped Ibarra or other Mexican-style chocolate, and finish with Manzanillo, or a salt infused with chiles.

CLASSIC PEANUT BRITTLE

Makes about ½ pound brittle

Peanut brittle is not hard to make, but it is hard to resist. I have to seriously limit its production for the sake of my waistline. Once made, it holds really well in the freezer. Put it in plastic zipper-top bags, and stash them way in the back of the freezer, under the frozen peas. If you don't, it won't be there for long. A glance at this recipe might lead you to believe that you don't actually need a large saucepan. Trust me—you do. Also, beware—sugar is hot. Very hot. Proceed with caution.

INGREDIENTS

½ cup light corn syrup

½ cup water

1 cup granulated sugar

1 cup peanuts, raw or blanched

2 tablespoons unsalted butter

1 teaspoon unrefined salt—*try Cyprus Pyramid, Maldon, a Japanese shio, Arabian fleur de sel, smoked salt, or a salt infused with sriracha, chocolate, vanilla, chile, or orange*

1 teaspoon pure vanilla extract

1 teaspoon baking soda

METHOD

1. Coat a large piece of aluminum foil or parchment paper with nonstick cooking spray. Set aside. In a large saucepan combine the corn syrup, water, and sugar. Set it over high heat and bring to a boil. When it is at the boil, add the peanuts and continue cooking until the sugar turns a deep golden caramel color, usually around 300°F.

2. Remove the saucepan from the heat and immediately stir in the butter, ½ teaspoon of the salt, the vanilla, and the baking soda. The mixture will foam up like Krakatoa (hence the large saucepan). When the foam reaches its maximum foaminess, pour the entire mixture out onto the prepared surface. Sprinkle immediately with remaining ½ teaspoon salt, then let cool for 3 to 5 minutes.

3. If you like the traditional brittle, which is superthin, begin carefully stretching it (with 2 forks, or your asbestos fingers) from the edges. Work your way around the edges, pulling off pieces as they cool. If you like a chunkier brittle, just let it cool as is, then crack it into chunks. (My friend Teri, a great cook and the photographer of this book, insists you must use a super-cute tiny brittle hammer for this. I have no such convictions, but the hammers are supercute.) Store the brittle, airtight, at room temperature for 2 days, or freeze for longer storage.

VARIATIONS

—Other Nut. This recipe makes fine brittle with whatever nut is your favorite. It even works with shredded coconut (choose unsweetened), sesame seeds, or sunflower seeds for the hippies among you.

—Spicy Brittle. Add cayenne pepper or your favorite hot sauce (to taste) along with the baking soda for a delectably spicy brittle. Then finish with a spicy infused salt.

—Citrus. Add the finely grated zest of 1 large orange, lemon, or lime with the baking soda for a refreshing citrus twist. You can finish it here with a citrus-infused salt.

CLASSIC PEANUT BRITTLE

TOFFEE WITH
WHITE CHOCOLATE
AND MACADAMIA

TOFFEE WITH WHITE CHOCOLATE AND MACADAMIA

Makes about ½ pound toffee

This recipe is a annual event at my house. If I don't have a bag stashed in the freezer when the kids come home for the holidays, all hell breaks loose. Be sure to see all the terrific variations. They'll help keep your freezer stocked with toffee for the foreseeable future.

INGREDIENTS

1¼ cups packed brown sugar

2 tablespoons water

8 tablespoons (1 stick/4 ounces) unsalted butter

¼ teaspoon baking soda

1 teaspoon pure vanilla extract

6 ounces white chocolate, chopped (or 1 cup chocolate chips)

1 cup chopped macadamia nuts

1 teaspoon Black Diamond or Black Lava salt

METHOD

1. Spread a large sheet of parchment or waxed paper out on your countertop and coat it with nonstick cooking spray. Coat a metal offset spatula with the spray as well, and have at the ready.

2. Combine the brown sugar, water, and butter in a large saucepan and bring to a boil over high heat. Continue to cook, stirring occasionally, until it reaches the hard-crack stage (285°F). When it's ready, it will start to smoke, but don't be alarmed. That's the flavor signal!

3. Immediately remove from the heat, add the baking soda and vanilla together, and stir them in until the mixture is very foamy. Immediately pour out onto the prepared paper and spread as thinly as possible, using the offset spatula. Work fast! This candy cools quickly!

4. Sprinkle the chopped chocolate across the surface of the toffee and let it stand for 5 minutes to melt. When the chocolate has melted, spread it thinly to cover the entire surface of the toffee. While the chocolate is still wet, sprinkle on the chopped nuts and the salt. Chill just until chocolate is set, then break into shards. Store finished, cooled candy airtight, at room temperature, or freeze in plastic zipper-top bags for prolonged storage (and snacks).

VARIATION

—Chocolate-Nut Combos. Any type of nut and chocolate will work on top of this toffee. Try dark chocolate with toasted pecans, almonds, coconut, or smashed candy canes and a good fleur de sel. Milk chocolate is perfect with hazelnuts, cashews, pepitas, or chopped candied orange. Then finish with pink Peruvian, Mayan, or Murray River salt. White chocolate is also nice with pistachios, toasted sesame, or toasted coconut, and any good Hawaiian salt. I'm sure you can think of some more ideas.

SMOKED PENUCHE FUDGE

Makes about 1 pound fudge

Penuche refers to the use of brown sugar in the absence of chocolate. The flavor is richer, "molasses-y," and has maple overtones. It is made not only into fudge, but also as a cake frosting (which is amazing on carrot cake). Some chefs think the name comes from the Spanish *panocha*, which means "raw sugar." But there are those penuche lovers in New England that swear it is named for 1920s Boston Bruin Mark Penuche, who liked maple syrup—a lot. (He brings Buddy the Elf to mind.) I fall on the side of the Bruins, because I think if it had come from the Spanish word, it would have been the Spanish word. I'm pretty sure people in the olden days could speak Spanish correctly.

INGREDIENTS

1½ cups granulated sugar

1 cup packed dark brown sugar

⅓ cup heavy cream

⅓ cup whole milk

2 tablespoons unsalted butter

1 teaspoon smoked salt, plus more for dusting—*try alder, hickory, apple, guava, Danish Viking, Halen Môn gold, or use your own home-smoked salt*

1 teaspoon pure vanilla extract or bourbon

½ cup smoked almonds

METHOD

1. Line a 9 x 5-inch loaf pan with aluminum foil, and coat it well with nonstick cooking spray. Lightly spray the sides of a large saucepan as well, then fill it with the granulated sugar, brown sugar, cream, and milk. Bring to a boil over medium-high heat, stirring, until sugars have melted. Insert a candy thermometer and cook, stirring occasionally, until the temperature registers 234 to 240°F (soft ball stage), 8 to 10 minutes. At this point, remove the saucepan from the heat, add the butter, and let it sit, unstirred, until the temperature reaches 110°F. (Check every 5 to 10 minutes—cooling rates will vary.)

2. Remove the thermometer, add the salt and the nuts, and beat with spoon until the mixture thickens and loses its shine. Immediately turn it out into the prepared pan and press it smooth, then sprinkle the top with additional smoked salt. While still hot, score the fudge into serving pieces, then cool completely. To serve, using the foil, lift the candy out of the pan and cut following the score marks. Store, airtight, at room temperature for a week, or freeze for longer storage.

VARIATIONS

—**Non-Smoker.** Forget the smoked salt and use any good flake or fleur de sel. Then use a nonsmoked almond, or any other nut, such as peanuts, pecans, or walnuts.

—**Chocolate.** For a chocolaty version, add 2 ounces unsweetened chocolate to the saucepan with the milk. Keep it smoky, or try it with no nuts and a fine pink rock salt.

—**Vanilla.** Use all white sugar, add 1 tablespoon corn syrup to the saucepan, and scrape a vanilla bean into the pan with the butter. Keep it smoky, or omit the nuts and try a Japanese plum salt, or a salt infused with vanilla.

SALTED
TRUFFLES

MILK-
CHOCOLATE
ANISE
CARAMELS

SMOKED
PENUCHE
FUDGE

SALTED TRUFFLES

Makes about 2 dozen truffles

Truffles are nothing but ganache, which is a basic culinary preparation every cook should know. It's super easy, and super versatile. Once you master it (which doesn't take long) the possibilities are endless. Use it as a filling for tarts, a frosting or glaze for cakes, thin it out for a sauce, or add milk for the best hot cocoa you ever had. It also makes a great late-night sugar fix. Just add a spoon.

INGREDIENTS

1 pound bittersweet chocolate

1 tablespoon unsalted butter

¼ teaspoon pure vanilla extract

1 teaspoon unrefined salt—*try Sal de Maras, Cyprus flake, Bali Pyramid, any good flake salt, a smoked salt, or a salt infused with matcha, vanilla, bourbon, red wine, lavender, rose, sweet spice, or orange*

1 cup heavy cream

METHOD

1. Chop the chocolate into small pieces. Add half of the chocolate to a clean dry bowl and set aside. Put the other half in a bowl along with the butter, vanilla, and ½ teaspoon of the salt. Warm the cream in a small saucepan over medium-high heat. As soon as it starts to boil, remove it from the heat and pour it over the chocolate-butter bowl. Shake the bowl so that that all the chocolate is submerged, then set aside, untouched, for 5 minutes.

2. At the 5-minute mark, whisk it until smooth. Set the ganache aside to set. At this point, you can refrigerate if you are in a hurry. As soon as the ganache is firm, form it into small balls, either by hand, or using a ⅙- to ¼-ounce ice cream scoop, and place on a parchment paper–lined baking sheet. Chill for 10 minutes.

3. Melt the remaining chocolate over a double boiler (see Glossary page 200). Have at the ready a trivet, or something to set the hot pot on, as well as a clean tray lined with parchment paper, and a few sheets of extra parchment paper. Remove the double boiler from the heat and set it on the trivet. Drop the chilled truffles into the melted chocolate. Coat with the chocolate and fish them out with a fork, then tap the fork on the edge of the pot, encouraging the excess chocolate to drip back into the pot. Now rub the fork along the extra sheets of parchment to clean excess chocolate off the foot (which is what we call the bottom of the truffle). Finally, place the dipped truffle on the clean, parchment paper–lined tray. Immediately sprinkle with another tiny pinch of salt. Repeat with the remaining balls of ganache. Because the chocolate is not tempered, store these truffles in the refrigerator until ready to serve. I like to serve them in small candy cups, or on a clean, dry salt block.

VARIATIONS

—Dip-Free. Instead of dipping the ganache balls in melted chocolate, you can serve them the original way, rolled in cocoa powder to simulate the dirt on the outside of the truffle fungus. (Leave it to the French to make dirt appealing.) You can also roll it in powdered sugar, finely ground espresso beans, finely ground toasted nuts, or toasted coconut. You can even mix your salt into these powders for an amazing effect.

—Spiced. There are a million other ways to flavor dark chocolate truffles, but with the salt I like to keep it simple. If you are really feeling exotic, though, try adding ½ teaspoon of cardamom, ground toasted anise, or your favorite chile powder.

VANILLA PANNA COTTA

Makes six 4-ounce servings

This is one of those desserts that make you feel powerful. It is superfancy, but supereasy. If vanilla is just too plain for you, see the variations for more flavor ideas than you can shake a stick at—or a bean, as it were.

INGREDIENTS

2 tablespoons water

2½ teaspoons (¼-ounce envelope) unflavored gelatin (or 4 sheets gelatin)

2 cups heavy cream

1 cup half-and-half

⅓ cup granulated sugar

1 vanilla bean, scraped

½ teaspoon unrefined salt—*try Maldon, fleur de sel, fiore di sale, or a salt infused with rose, citrus, vanilla, chocolate, espresso, lavender, sesame, anise, or cognac*

METHOD

1. Place the water in a small bowl, and sprinkle the gelatin on top. Let it sit for 5 minutes, until the water has been absorbed and the gelatin has bloomed. (If using sheet gelatin, increase the water and soak the sheets, submerged, for 1 to 2 minutes.) Prepare individual 4-ounce molds with a light coating of nonstick cooking spray. (I usually spray, then wipe out the excess, so nothing but a thin film remains.)

2. Combine the heavy cream, half-and-half, sugar, vanilla bean, and salt in a medium saucepan. Place over medium heat and bring to a simmer. Stir until the sugar has dissolved, then remove from the heat. Add the bloomed gelatin (or squeezed-out limp sheets) to the warm cream and stir until completely dissolved. Pour the mixture into the prepared mold, and chill for 1 hour, or until firm. (Overnight is fine, too.)

3. To unmold, wet your thumb and run it around the top of the custard, where it attaches to the mold. Press down to let some air into the bottom, which will break the vacuum. Unmold onto serving plates and serve with fresh seasonal fruit and a final sprinkle of the salt.

VARIATIONS

—Infused Cream. As you may have guessed, flavor best enters panna cotta via infusion with the cream. When added this way, the ingredients will not alter the preferred, creamy texture of the finished product. For this reason, the best flavors to use include toasted nuts, coffee, tea (matcha, hojicha, chai, Earl Grey), spices (cinnamon stick, star anise, crushed cardamom pods), herbs (lavender, thyme, mint, basil) or citrus zest (try lemon with rosemary). All of these can be added to the warm cream, steeped for several hours, or overnight, and then strained out. Potent extracts work, too, but be careful, as their flavors are usually obviously artificial. For best results, consider mixing them with a natural flavor. Try almond and orange flower water, or saffron and rose water.

—Puree Additions. For flavors that have some texture, like pumpkin puree, strawberry jam, or goat cheese, some adjustments will need to be made. Add no more than a cup, and increase the gelatin by half again as much (for a total of 3¾ teaspoons, 1½ packets, or 6 sheets).

—Savory. Omit the sugar and vanilla to make a savory cream for an amazing appetizer or side dish. Try corn, chunky shrimp, roasted chiles, dried mushrooms, or foie gras.

NO-CHURN SALTED CHOCOLATE ICE CREAM

Makes about 1 quart ice cream

I am a firm believer that everyone needs to make homemade ice cream. There is nothing better under the sun, especially when the sun is working overtime. This no-churn recipe makes homemade ice cream accessible to everyone. (In case you missed it, I wrote a whole book on the subject.) The basic recipe is based on the French *parfait*, a custard that is frozen into a loaf shape and sliced like a sweet terrine. The results will surprise you, and you'll be hooked on the technique—I guarantee it.

INGREDIENTS

1 cup bittersweet chocolate, chopped (or bittersweet chocolate chips)

1 cup whole milk

One 13-ounce can sweetened condensed milk

1 teaspoon pure vanilla extract

1 tablespoon unsweetened cocoa powder

1 tablespoon fresh lemon juice

1 teaspoon unrefined salt—*try Maldon, Halen Môn, Cyprus Flake, fleur de sel, a smoked salt, or a salt infused with chocolate, vanilla, orange, bourbon, cognac, matcha, espresso, cinnamon, bacon, maple, sesame, or hot chiles*

2 cups heavy cream

METHOD

1. Place the chopped chocolate in a large heat-proof bowl. Bring the milk to a near boil, then pour it over the chopped chocolate in the bowl. Let sit for 5 minutes, then stir until smooth. Stir in sweetened condensed milk, vanilla, cocoa powder, lemon juice, and ½ teaspoon of the salt.

2. In a separate bowl, whip the heavy cream until it reaches soft peaks. Fold the cream gently into the chocolate-milk mixture, then transfer to a freezable container. Sprinkle the top with remaining ½ teaspoon salt, then cover with plastic wrap pressed directly on the surface of the custard. (This prevents ice crystals from ruining your creamy texture.) Place in the freezer for about 6 hours, or until firm and scoopable. (FYI: thinner layers freeze faster!) Serve scoops any way you like, but don't forget an extra pinch of the salt.

VARIATIONS

—Vanilla. Omit the chocolate, add a scraped vanilla bean to the milk, and use Black Diamond, Black Lava, or a Japanese plum salt.

—Fruity Ice Cream. Make a vanilla base, as above, and before folding in the whipped cream, fold in about 1 cup of your favorite fruit puree or jam. The thicker the puree the better. Finish the fruity recipes with any Hawaiian salt, a bamboo salt, or a smoked salt. (For more no-churn ideas, see my book, *No-Churn Ice Cream*.)

JAL JEERA POPSICLES

Makes a dozen tiny popsicles

This cooling Indian herbed lemonade, the name of which means "cumin water," is a summer necessity in India. It also works well as an aperitif, stimulating the appetite for what's to come (presumably tons of amazing curries). It is this property that I like to harness as a palate cleanser. Made into tiny popsicles and served after dinner, but before dessert, they pave the way for a richer, sweeter final dessert course. It's also pretty great enjoyed as the traditional iced tea, or as a normal, large popsicle. Preferably by a pool. Incidentally, I like to use natural sticks instead of popsicle sticks. Try lemon tree branches, thin cinnamon sticks, or short lengths of lemongrass.

INGREDIENTS

½ cup fresh mint leaves, chopped

½ cup fresh cilantro leaves, chopped

1 tablespoon peeled and grated fresh ginger

½ teaspoon cumin seeds, toasted and ground

½ teaspoon fennel seeds, toasted and ground

½ teaspoon amchoor powder (see Glossary page 199)

½ teaspoon freshly ground black pepper

1 black cardamom pod, seeds removed, and crushed

1 pinch ground asafetida

1 teaspoon Kala Namak (Indian Black Salt)

Finely grated zest of 1 lemon

¼ cup honey

1 tablespoon tamarind paste

4 cups water

¼ cup fresh lemon juice

Crushed ice

METHOD

1. Using a mortar and pestle or a food processor, blend the mint, cilantro, ginger, cumin, fennel, amchoor, pepper, cardamom, asafetida, and salt to a coarse paste. Add the honey and tamarind paste and process until smooth. Transfer the mixture to a pitcher and stir in the water and lemon juice. Set aside to steep for 30 minutes.

2. Strain the mixture, then pour into popsicle molds or Dixie cups and insert sticks. If you are using Dixie cups, fill, cover with plastic wrap, then insert the sticks through the plastic to hold them in place. Freeze until solid, about 4 hours. To serve as iced tea, pour over crushed ice and serve with a dusting of chaat masala.

NO-CHURN MELON MINT SORBET

Makes about 1 quart

In the early summer a large variety of melons begin to flood the market. Canary, Crenshaw, Casaba, Santa Claus, Sharlyn, Persian—and there are probably other specialty varieties in your area. Try them all with this recipe. Then try it again. The varying levels of sweetness throughout the summer will make it new every time.

INGREDIENTS

1 cup honey

1 cup water

1 cup chopped fresh mint leaves

4 cups melon chunks, peeled and seeded

Finely grated zest and juice of 1 small lime

½ teaspoon unrefined salt—*try Mayan, Manzanillo, Persian Blue, Hawaiian, or a salt infused with mint, sriracha, chipotle, citrus, ginger, curry, saffron, or peppercorns*

METHOD

1. Combine the honey, water, and mint in a small saucepan. Place over high heat and bring to a boil. Reduce to a simmer and cook for 5 minutes. Remove from the heat and let cool completely. (You can do this a day before.)

2. Add the melon, lime zest, and lime juice to the bowl of a bar blender or food processor and process until smooth. Very slowly pour in the honey-mint syrup, adding only ¼ cup at a time, and tasting periodically, as the different sugar levels of the melons will vary. When the flavor is just right, transfer the mixture to a shallow freezable container.

3. Sprinkle the surface with the salt, then cover loosely with plastic wrap or waxed paper and place in the freezer. Stir the mixture every 30 minutes until it starts to hold its shape. In about 4 hours it will have attained a scoopable consistency.

4. Scoop into chilled glasses or bowls and serve with a mixed melon ball salad (try adding peppercorns and tarragon or mint), fresh berries and yogurt, a peppercorn caramel glaze, chopped prosciutto, salty meringues, or a shot of vodka.

SALTED CARAMEL SAUCE

Makes about 3 cups

The world is abuzz with salted caramel, which is funny, because it has been a thing in France for decades. They tried it in London, to turned-up noses. But once the Americans started doing it—instant trend. (Once the cool kids are in, everyone wants in.) This recipe is a must-have. It will keep for weeks in the refrigerator and can be embellished to suit your mood. (See the variations below.)

INGREDIENTS

2 cups granulated sugar

¼ cup water

1 tablespoon fresh lemon juice

1½ cups heavy cream

4 tablespoons (½ stick/2 ounces) unsalted butter

1 to 2 teaspoons unrefined salt—*try Japanese shio, Cyprus flake, Maldon, a smoked salt, or a salt infused with vanilla, bourbon, cognac, anise, bacon, palm sugar, maple, chocolate, or citrus*

METHOD

1. In a large saucepan, combine the sugar and the water. Mix it together well, wipe all stray sugar crystals off the insides of pan with wet hands, or a pastry brush, and place the pan over high heat. Cook, without moving or stirring.

2. When the mixture reaches a rolling boil, add the lemon juice into the center of the pot. Do not stir. Continue cooking until the sugar is a dark, golden amber (between 320 and 350°F on a candy thermometer).

3. Immediately remove from the heat and carefully whisk in the cream. Be careful here. The cream will cause the caramel to erupt like Mentos in Diet Coke. (Some cooks like to wear an oven mitt while whisking at this stage.) Once the bubbles have subsided, add the butter and half of the salt, and whisk until smooth. Taste and add more salt as you deem fit. Cool the sauce to room temperature. Store, airtight, for several weeks in the refrigerator.

VARIATION

—**Flavored Caramel.** Any number of flavor additions can be made after the caramel sauce is complete. Try adding vanilla bean, citrus zest, orange liqueur, espresso, peanut butter, melted chocolate, or coconut milk.

—**Browned Butter.** I love the flavor of browned butter. Melt butter in a saucepan and let it continue to cook until the bubbles subside, the solids fall to the bottom of the pan, and the melted butter turns from brown to black (It might smoke a bit, but remember—smoke is the flavor sign! Remove from the heat, let cool slightly, then make your caramel sauce. When it's time to add the butter, add the browned butter, being sure to scrape all the little black bits from the bottom of the pan.

—**Clear Caramel Glaze.** For a totally different look, add water or another clear liquid in place of the cream. This makes a beautiful see-through sauce that allows you to feature floating flavor additives. It looks amazing with a vanilla bean, any ground spices, whole seeds (anise, fennel, sesame), flowers, tea leaves, coffee grounds, and, of course, chunky salts.

VARIATIONS

—**Sweet Fruit Lassi.** Add a cup of fresh chopped mango, strawberries, bananas, or a mixture, and a pinch of saffron, cardamom, or a few drops of rose water

—**Salted Mint Lassi.** Replace the curry leaves with mint and add 1 teaspoon of peeled and grated fresh ginger.

—**Just Drink It.** You can serve this mixture straight out of the blender, over crushed ice, as is traditional.

KHARA LASSI GRANITA

Makes about 1 quart granita

Lassi is a classic Indian drink that cools the heat of an Indian meal. But it makes a great frozen dessert, too. Frozen and stirred periodically, the resulting crystals are incredibly refreshing. There are several versions of a lassi, so check the variations for your favorite.

INGREDIENTS

1 cup plain yogurt

¼ cup honey

2 cups cold water

1 teaspoon Kala Namak (Indian Black Salt)

Pinch of ground cumin or asafetida

4 curry leaves

Optional garnishes: ground cumin, a sprig of mint or curry leaf, a lime wedge and a slice of mango

METHOD

1. Combine all the ingredients in a blender and process until frothy. Pour through a fine-mesh strainer into a shallow baking dish. Place it in the freezer and stir every 20 minutes with a fork, until the entire pan is frozen and slushy, 1½ to 2 hours. Serve in chilled glasses with a dusting of ground cumin, a sprig of mint or curry leaf, or a wedge of lime and a slice of mango.

CRISP SALTY MERINGUES

Makes about 2 dozen meringues

The most challenging aspect of this dessert is regulating your oven to a low enough temperature. Too hot, they will turn brown and weep (much like I do when they turn out this way).

If you can, dry them in a dehydrator overnight. It is less temperamental, and they always come out white.

INGREDIENTS

1 cup large egg whites (about 8)

½ teaspoon cream of tartar

1½ cups granulated sugar

4 ounces bittersweet chocolate, grated (on a standard box cheese grater)

1 tablespoon unrefined salt—*try Black Diamond, Black Lava, Murray River, Haleakala red alaea, smoked salt, or a salt infused with matcha, rose, citrus, chocolate, coffee, sesame, or hot chiles*

METHOD

1. Preheat the oven to 200°F. Line a baking sheet with parchment paper and coat lightly with nonstick cooking spray.

2. Combine the egg whites and cream of tartar in the bowl of a stand mixer fitted with the whip attachment. (Or use a regular bowl and a balloon whisk.) Whip to soft peaks, then slowly rain in the sugar, 1 tablespoon at a time, until the peaks are stiff and all the sugar has been added. Remove the bowl from the machine and carefully fold in the chocolate and the salt.

3. Scoop or pipe mounds of the meringue on the prepared pan, spacing them 1 inch apart. Transfer to the oven and bake for 1 hour. Then turn the oven off, prop the oven door open slightly, and let them sit for several hours, until dry and crisp. Store the meringues, airtight, at room temperature, for several days, or freeze for longer storage.

VARIATIONS

—**Chocolate-Free.** Omit the chocolate for a plain one.

glossary

ACKEE/ACKEE FRUIT. The national fruit of Jamaica, the ackee was brought from West Africa, most likely onboard a slave ship. It is in the same family as the lychee, and like the lychee, it is only the light flesh surrounding the pit that is used. Used more like a vegetable than a fruit, it takes on an "eggy" quality when cooked. It is best known as a crucial element in Jamaica's national dish, Ackee and Salt Fish. Ackee is only legally available canned in the U.S.

AMCHOOR. A beige powder made from dried green mango, added to Indian dishes for its tangy, sour, acidic nature. Also known as mango powder.

ANISE. The seed from a flowering plant in the carrot family, native to the Mediterranean region. The flavor is similar to licorice and fennel, and star anise, but all are from different botanical families.

BAHĀRĀT. Each spice merchant has a different version of this Middle Eastern spice blend, but it typically contains some variation of allspice, pepper, cardamom, cinnamon, cloves, cumin, nutmeg, and chiles.

BÂTON. In culinary terms this French word for short stick or rod refers to the basis for the classic dice cut. Technically it should measure ¼ x ¼ x 3 inches.

BLANCH. To boil briefly, then submerge in ice water to halt the cooking and set the color. The process is used to lightly cook and brighten vegetables, and to loosen the skin of tomatoes and stone fruits. It is also referred to as parboiling.

BOUQUET GARNI. This is the classic French culinary procedure of tying together a few aromatics—usually sprigs of parsley, thyme, and bay— either with string or wrapped in cheesecloth. The purpose is to flavor liquid preparations (broths, soups, stews) in a way that will let you easily retrieve the herbs when the cooking is complete.

BRANDADE. A classic dish from the Languedoc and Provence regions of France, consisting of pureed salt cod, olive oil, garlic, and cream, spread on toasted bread. Similar variations appear throughout the Basque Region, Spain, Portugal, and Italy, often with added potato.

BRIQUETAGE. A ceramic material used to make evaporation vessels for the manufacture of salt during the Bronze Age in Europe. The vessels, which had to be broken to access the salt, were then discarded in piles. Salt-making sites can be identified by hills that have covered and concealed the piles over the centuries. These hills have taken on a red hue from the broken ceramic vessels that lie underneath. Composition of these vessels varied from site to site, and archeologists have used this information to identify trade networks.

BROWNED BUTTER. This is melted butter, known also as *beurre noisette*, or the darker *beurre noir*, that is allowed to cook until the solids sink to the bottom of the pan and begin to caramelize. The dark-colored solids contain all the flavor, and the darker they are, even to the point of black as in *beurre noir*, the more delightful the flavor is. Used in recipes, or poured as is over vegetables.

BUTTERFLY. A butchering term that denotes cutting a food through the center. The two halves are not detached, but rather, the food is opened up like butterfly wings to create a larger, thinner portion.

CACAO NIBS. These are cocoa beans that have been roasted, hulled, and crushed. Used as an add-in for chocolate confections, they are only a couple of steps away from being chocolate. You can make chocolate by processing the nibs into a paste and adding sugar.

CAPSICUM/CAPSAICIN. This is the compound that makes chiles hot. It is found mainly in the seeds and membrane of the chiles, and removing these is the only way to diminish the heat. The seeds and membrane transfer the volatile oils to everything they touch, so one should wear gloves when seeding chiles. If your hands touch this oil, they will, in turn, transfer it to everything they touch.

artisan salt purveyors

There are many places that will sell you fancy salts. There are only two I patronize. Their prices are fair and their assortments are outstanding.

THE MEADOW. Mark Bitterman offers the best assortment of salts, beautifully packaged and at reasonable prices. He chooses the best from around the world and sells them in a variety of sizes, separately, and in large and small tasting sets. He also sells salt blocks. There area few people as salt-smart as Mr. Bitterman, and the employees at his brick and mortar stores are equally knowledgeable. You can order any of their salts online, too, as well as an impressive collection of chocolate and bitters.

3731 North Mississippi Ave.	805 Northwest 23rd Ave.	523 Hudson Street
Portland, OR 97227	Portland, OR 97210	New York, NY 10014
		themeadow.com

KALUSTYAN'S. This is the one place I must visit every time I am in New York City, even if I am only in town for a day. They have a huge selection of salts from around the world at really good prices. They are not packaged as prettily as the salts at The Meadow, but who cares. They carry some salts that The Meadow does not, including local NYC-rooftop salt, which is superfun. They also have every spice you will ever need, cooking tools, and exotic prepared foods. Happily, everything is also available online.

123 Lexington Ave.
New York, NY, 10016
Kalustyans.com

acknowledgments

A gigantic thank-you goes out to everyone at SMP, but especially to my editor, BJ Berti, who, though she thought she was just having lunch, willingly submitted to a poolside salt tasting. And of course, hugs to my agent, Katherine Latshaw, who is ever supportive.

index